ATTILA

ATTILA

Steven Béla Várdy

CHELSEA HOUSE PUBLISHERS
NEW YORK
PHILADELPHIA

Chelsea House Publishers
EDITOR-IN-CHIEF: Remmel Nunn
MANAGING EDITOR: Karyn Gullen Browne
COPY CHIEF: Juliann Barbato
PICTURE EDITOR: Adrian G. Allen
ART DIRECTOR: Maria Epes
DEPUTY COPY CHIEF: Mark Rifkin
ASSISTANT ART DIRECTOR: Noreen Romano
MANUFACTURING MANAGER: Gerald Levine
SYSTEMS MANAGER: Lindsey Ottman
PRODUCTION MANAGER: Joseph Romano
PRODUCTION COORDINATOR: Marie Claire Cebrián

World Leaders—Past & Present
SENIOR EDITOR: John W. Selfridge

Staff for ATTILA
ASSOCIATE EDITOR: Jeff Klein
COPY EDITOR: Philip Koslow
EDITORIAL ASSISTANT: Martin Mooney
PICTURE RESEARCHER: Alan Gottlieb
DESIGNER: David Murray
ASSISTANT DESIGNER: Diana Blume

First Printing

1 3 5 7 9 8 6 4 2

Library of Congress Cataloging-in-Publication Data

Várdy, Steven Béla.
    Attila the Hun/Steven Béla Várdy.
    p.   cm.—(World leaders—past and present)
    Includes bibliographical references and index.
    Summary: Surveys the life and times of Attila, king of the Huns,
and discusses his image in myth and history.
    ISBN 1-55546-803-9
          0-7910-0691-3 (pbk.)
    1. Attila, d. 453—Juvenile literature. 2. Huns—Biography—
Juvenile literature. 3. Huns—History—Juvenile literature. [1. Attila,
d. 453. 2. Kings, queens, rulers, etc. 3. Huns—History.] I. Title.
II. Series.
D141.V37   1991
936'.0099—dc20   90–40544
[B]   CIP
[92]   AC

Contents

WORLD LEADERS PAST & PRESENT

John Adams
John Quincy Adams
Konrad Adenauer
Alexander the Great
Salvador Allende
Marc Antony
Corazon Aquino
Yasir Arafat
King Arthur
Hafez al-Assad
Kemal Atatürk
Attila
Clement Attlee
Augustus Caesar
Menachem Begin
David Ben-Gurion
Otto von Bismarck
Léon Blum
Simon Bolívar
Cesare Borgia
Willy Brandt
Leonid Brezhnev
Julius Caesar
John Calvin
Jimmy Carter
Fidel Castro
Catherine the Great
Charlemagne
Chiang Kai-Shek
Winston Churchill
Georges Clemenceau
Cleopatra
Constantine the Great
Hernán Cortés
Oliver Cromwell
Georges-Jacques
  Danton
Jefferson Davis
Moshe Dayan
Charles de Gaulle
Eamon De Valera
Eugene Debs
Deng Xiaoping
Benjamin Disraeli
Alexander Dubček
François & Jean-Claude
  Duvalier
Dwight Eisenhower
Eleanor of Aquitaine
Elizabeth I
Faisal
Ferdinand & Isabella
Francisco Franco
Benjamin Franklin

Frederick the Great
Indira Gandhi
Mohandas Gandhi
Giuseppe Garibaldi
Amin & Bashir Gemayel
Genghis Khan
William Gladstone
Mikhail Gorbachev
Ulysses S. Grant
Ernesto "Che" Guevara
Tenzin Gyatso
Alexander Hamilton
Dag Hammarskjöld
Henry VIII
Henry of Navarre
Paul von Hindenburg
Hirohito
Adolf Hitler
Ho Chi Minh
King Hussein
Ivan the Terrible
Andrew Jackson
James I
Wojciech Jaruzelski
Thomas Jefferson
Joan of Arc
Pope John XXIII
Pope John Paul II
Lyndon Johnson
Benito Juárez
John Kennedy
Robert Kennedy
Jomo Kenyatta
Ayatollah Khomeini
Nikita Khrushchev
Kim Il Sung
Martin Luther King, Jr.
Henry Kissinger
Kublai Khan
Lafayette
Robert E. Lee
Vladimir Lenin
Abraham Lincoln
David Lloyd George
Louis XIV
Martin Luther
Judas Maccabeus
James Madison
Nelson & Winnie
  Mandela
Mao Zedong
Ferdinand Marcos
George Marshall

Mary, Queen of Scots
Tomáš Masaryk
Golda Meir
Klemens von Metternich
James Monroe
Hosni Mubarak
Robert Mugabe
Benito Mussolini
Napoléon Bonaparte
Gamal Abdel Nasser
Jawaharlal Nehru
Nero
Nicholas II
Richard Nixon
Kwame Nkrumah
Daniel Ortega
Mohammed Reza Pahlavi
Thomas Paine
Charles Stewart
  Parnell
Pericles
Juan Perón
Peter the Great
Pol Pot
Muammar el-Qaddafi
Ronald Reagan
Cardinal Richelieu
Maximilien Robespierre
Eleanor Roosevelt
Franklin Roosevelt
Theodore Roosevelt
Anwar Sadat
Haile Selassie
Prince Sihanouk
Jan Smuts
Joseph Stalin
Sukarno
Sun Yat-sen
Tamerlane
Mother Teresa
Margaret Thatcher
Josip Broz Tito
Toussaint L'Ouverture
Leon Trotsky
Pierre Trudeau
Harry Truman
Queen Victoria
Lech Walesa
George Washington
Chaim Weizmann
Woodrow Wilson
Xerxes
Emiliano Zapata
Zhou Enlai

CHELSEA HOUSE PUBLISHERS

ON LEADERSHIP

Arthur M. Schlesinger, jr.

LEADERSHIP, it may be said, is really what makes the world go round. Love no doubt smooths the passage; but love is a private transaction between consenting adults. Leadership is a public transaction with history. The idea of leadership affirms the capacity of individuals to move, inspire, and mobilize masses of people so that they act together in pursuit of an end. Sometimes leadership serves good purposes, sometimes bad; but whether the end is benign or evil, great leaders are those men and women who leave their personal stamp on history.

Now, the very concept of leadership implies the proposition that individuals can make a difference. This proposition has never been universally accepted. From classical times to the present day, eminent thinkers have regarded individuals as no more than the agents and pawns of larger forces, whether the gods and goddesses of the ancient world or, in the modern era, race, class, nation, the dialectic, the will of the people, the spirit of the times, history itself. Against such forces, the individual dwindles into insignificance.

So contends the thesis of historical determinism. Tolstoy's great novel *War and Peace* offers a famous statement of the case. Why, Tolstoy asked, did millions of men in the Napoleonic Wars, denying their human feelings and their common sense, move back and forth across Europe slaughtering their fellows? "The war," Tolstoy answered, "was bound to happen simply because it was bound to happen." All prior history predetermined it. As for leaders, they, Tolstoy said, "are but the labels that serve to give a name to an end and, like labels, they have the least possible connection with the event." The greater the leader, "the more conspicuous the inevitability and the predestination of every act he commits." The leader, said Tolstoy, is "the slave of history."

Determinism takes many forms. Marxism is the determinism of class. Nazism the determinism of race. But the idea of men and women as the slaves of history runs athwart the deepest human instincts. Rigid determinism abolishes the idea of human freedom—

the assumption of free choice that underlies every move we make, every word we speak, every thought we think. It abolishes the idea of human responsibility, since it is manifestly unfair to reward or punish people for actions that are by definition beyond their control. No one can live consistently by any deterministic creed. The Marxist states prove this themselves by their extreme susceptibility to the cult of leadership.

More than that, history refutes the idea that individuals make no difference. In December 1931 a British politician crossing Park Avenue in New York City between 76th and 77th Streets around 10:30 P.M. looked in the wrong direction and was knocked down by an automobile—a moment, he later recalled, of a man aghast, a world aglare: "I do not understand why I was not broken like an eggshell or squashed like a gooseberry." Fourteen months later an American politician, sitting in an open car in Miami, Florida, was fired on by an assassin; the man beside him was hit. Those who believe that individuals make no difference to history might well ponder whether the next two decades would have been the same had Mario Constasino's car killed Winston Churchill in 1931 and Giuseppe Zangara's bullet killed Franklin Roosevelt in 1933. Suppose, in addition, that Adolf Hitler had been killed in the street fighting during the Munich *Putsch* of 1923 and that Lenin had died of typhus during World War I. What would the 20th century be like now?

For better or for worse, individuals do make a difference. "The notion that a people can run itself and its affairs anonymously," wrote the philosopher William James, "is now well known to be the silliest of absurdities. Mankind does nothing save through initiatives on the part of inventors, great or small, and imitation by the rest of us—these are the sole factors in human progress. Individuals of genius show the way, and set the patterns, which common people then adopt and follow."

Leadership, James suggests, means leadership in thought as well as in action. In the long run, leaders in thought may well make the greater difference to the world. But, as Woodrow Wilson once said, "Those only are leaders of men, in the general eye, who lead in action. . . . It is at their hands that new thought gets its translation into the crude language of deeds." Leaders in thought often invent in solitude and obscurity, leaving to later generations the tasks of imitation. Leaders in action—the leaders portrayed in this series—have to be effective in their own time.

And they cannot be effective by themselves. They must act in response to the rhythms of their age. Their genius must be adapted, in a phrase of William James's, "to the receptivities of the moment." Leaders are useless without followers. "There goes the mob," said the French politician hearing a clamor in the streets. "I am their leader. I must follow them." Great leaders turn the inchoate emotions of the mob to purposes of their own. They seize on the opportunities of their time, the hopes, fears, frustrations, crises, potentialities. They succeed when events have prepared the way for them, when the community is awaiting to be aroused, when they can provide the clarifying and organizing ideas. Leadership ignites the circuit between the individual and the mass and thereby alters history.

It may alter history for better or for worse. Leaders have been responsible for the most extravagant follies and most monstrous crimes that have beset suffering humanity. They have also been vital in such gains as humanity has made in individual freedom, religious and racial tolerance, social justice, and respect for human rights.

There is no sure way to tell in advance who is going to lead for good and who for evil. But a glance at the gallery of men and women in *World Leaders—Past and Present* suggests some useful tests.

One test is this: Do leaders lead by force or by persuasion? By command or by consent? Through most of history leadership was exercised by the divine right of authority. The duty of followers was to defer and to obey. "Theirs not to reason why / Theirs but to do and die." On occasion, as with the so-called enlightened despots of the 18th century in Europe, absolutist leadership was animated by humane purposes. More often, absolutism nourished the passion for domination, land, gold, and conquest and resulted in tyranny.

The great revolution of modern times has been the revolution of equality. The idea that all people should be equal in their legal condition has undermined the old structure of authority, hierarchy, and deference. The revolution of equality has had two contrary effects on the nature of leadership. For equality, as Alexis de Tocqueville pointed out in his great study *Democracy in America*, might mean equality in servitude as well as equality in freedom.

"I know of only two methods of establishing equality in the political world," Tocqueville wrote. "Rights must be given to every citizen, or none at all to anyone . . . save one, who is the master of all." There was no middle ground "between the sovereignty of all and the absolute power of one man." In his astonishing prediction of 20th-century totalitarian dictatorship, Tocqueville explained how the revolution of equality could lead to the *"Führerprinzip"* and more terrible absolutism than the world had ever known.

But when rights are given to every citizen and the sovereignty of all is established, the problem of leadership takes a new form, becomes more exacting than ever before. It is easy to issue commands and enforce them by the rope and the stake, the concentration camp and the *gulag.* It is much harder to use argument and achievement to overcome opposition and win consent. The Founding Fathers of the United States understood the difficulty. They believed that history had given them the opportunity to decide, as Alexander Hamilton wrote in the first Federalist Paper, whether men are indeed capable of basing government on "reflection and choice, or whether they are forever destined to depend . . . on accident and force."

Government by reflection and choice called for a new style of leadership and a new quality of followership. It required leaders to be responsive to popular concerns, and it required followers to be active and informed participants in the process. Democracy does not eliminate emotion from politics; sometimes it fosters demagoguery; but it is confident that, as the greatest of democratic leaders put it, you cannot fool all of the people all of the time. It measures leadership by results and retires those who overreach or falter or fail.

It is true that in the long run despots are measured by results too. But they can postpone the day of judgment, sometimes indefinitely, and in the meantime they can do infinite harm. It is also true that democracy is no guarantee of virtue and intelligence in government, for the voice of the people is not necessarily the voice of God. But democracy, by assuring the right of opposition, offers built-in resistance to the evils inherent in absolutism. As the theologian Reinhold Niebuhr summed it up, "Man's capacity for justice makes democracy possible, but man's inclination to injustice makes democracy necessary."

A second test for leadership is the end for which power is sought. When leaders have as their goal the supremacy of a master race or the promotion of totalitarian revolution or the acquisition and exploitation of colonies or the protection of greed and privilege or the preservation of personal power, it is likely that their leadership will do little to advance the cause of humanity. When their goal is the abolition of slavery, the liberation of women, the enlargement of opportunity for the poor and powerless, the extension of equal rights to racial minorities, the defense of the freedoms of expression and opposition, it is likely that their leadership will increase the sum of human liberty and welfare.

Leaders have done great harm to the world. They have also conferred great benefits. You will find both sorts in this series. Even "good" leaders must be regarded with a certain wariness. Leaders are not demigods; they put on their trousers one leg after another just like ordinary mortals. No leader is infallible, and every leader needs to be reminded of this at regular intervals. Irreverence irritates leaders but is their salvation. Unquestioning submission corrupts leaders and demeans followers. Making a cult of a leader is always a mistake. Fortunately hero worship generates its own antidote. "Every hero," said Emerson, "becomes a bore at last."

The signal benefit the great leaders confer is to embolden the rest of us to live according to our own best selves, to be active, insistent, and resolute in affirming our own sense of things. For great leaders attest to the reality of human freedom against the supposed inevitabilities of history. And they attest to the wisdom and power that may lie within the most unlikely of us, which is why Abraham Lincoln remains the supreme example of great leadership. A great leader, said Emerson, exhibits new possibilities to all humanity. "We feed on genius. . . . Great men exist that there may be greater men."

Great leaders, in short, justify themselves by emancipating and empowering their followers. So humanity struggles to master its destiny, remembering with Alexis de Tocqueville: "It is true that around every man a fatal circle is traced beyond which he cannot pass; but within the wide verge of that circle he is powerful and free; as it is with man, so with communities."

1

The Death of a World Conqueror

Attila, the great Hunnic conqueror, was laid out under a huge embroidered silken tent whose sides had been folded up. His royal attendants, generals, and chief priests wanted to let his people see him once more before taking him to his final resting place.

The location of his tomb was to be kept secret. His sons and the other leaders of his empire wished to prevent anyone from ever finding and desecrating his grave. The remains of Attila, king of the Huns, Scourge of God, possessor of the Sacred Sword, and supreme ruler of a domain that stretched from the frontiers of the two Roman empires in southern and western Europe to central Asia beyond the Ural Mountains, were not to fall prey to the avarice of future generations. His tomb was to be hidden for all eternity, and no one — except those who were selected to join him in the world beyond — was to accompany him to his final resting place.

The Huns exceed anything that can be imagined in ferocity and barbarism. They gash their children's cheeks to prevent their beards growing. Their stocky body, huge arms, and disproportionally large head give them a monstrous appearance. They live like beasts.
—AMMIANUS MARCELLINUS
Roman soldier
and historian

A Hunnic warrior, depicted on an urn found in a king's grave. After Attila's death, the Huns took great care to keep his burial place secret. The slaves who assisted in the burial were killed to prevent them from revealing the location of the grave.

Attila's death came as unexpectedly as a thunderbolt out of a clear blue sky. It followed his marriage to Ildikó, the beautiful daughter of one of his vassal kings, in A.D. 453. Amid the merriment of the wedding celebration, Attila and his new wife retired into the nuptial chamber of the king's wooden palace.

The merrymaking continued throughout the night and into the next day. The drunken Huns awaited the return of their king from his chamber, but the day wore on and Attila did not emerge. Finally, his attendants broke into his royal quarters.

There they found the lifeless body of their king

Attila was suffocated by a severe nosebleed during his marriage feast. In this 19th-century German engraving, he is mourned by his bride, Ildikó, while his horrified followers discover his lifeless body in the nuptial chamber of the royal palace.

on his blood-soaked bed, his young bride next to him weeping silently under her veil. King Attila, ruler of Hunnia, was dead, but there were no signs of any violence upon his body. Apparently he had died of suffocation, choked to death by a severe nose-bleed while intoxicated.

"Worn out by excessive merriment," wrote the Byzantine historian Priscus, who had visited Attila in the Hunnic capital, "and sodden with sleep and wine he lay on his back. In this position a hemorrhage . . . poured down his throat in deadly passage and killed . . . [this] king famed in war."

Inevitably, rumors started to circulate claiming that Attila did not die a natural death but was killed in his sleep by his new bride. According to these stories, Ildikó slew her husband out of revenge for the indignities suffered by her father and two brothers at Attila's hands. These tales were later incorporated into various chronicles, such as the 6th-century chronicle of Marcellinus Comes, as well as several 9th- to 12th-century Nordic sagas.

Such gossip continued unabated even though it was denied by Attila's own sons, who were convinced that their father had died a natural death. Certainly, the great 14th-century English poet Geoffrey Chaucer did not believe these rumors, even though his description of Attila's death in his "Pardoner's Tale" is less than flattering:

Loke, Attila, the grete conquerour,
Deyde in his sleep, with shame and dishonor,
Bledinge ay at the nose in dronkenesse;
A capitayn shoulde live in sobrenesse.

The news of Attila's death spread quickly to all parts of Europe and Asia, bringing sorrow to his followers and delight to his enemies. According to legend, the ruler of the Byzantine, or Eastern Roman, Empire, Marcian, learned about Attila's demise on the very night of his death. On that night Emperor Marcian had a dream in which a divinity showed him the broken royal bow of the much-feared Attila. From this dream, Emperor Marcian supposedly concluded that his great rival had died and thus that his empire was finally free from conquest by the powerful barbarian ruler.

Equally interesting is the report by one of Attila's late-medieval biographers, Callimachus, who claims that for 21 days before Attila's death a huge comet illuminated the sky over his empire. People were convinced that this signaled the coming of an event of universal significance, although they did not know what the event would be. Then, on the day of Attila's marriage to Ildikó, his favorite stallion died unexpectedly. Soon after that the king himself stumbled and fell just as he was about to enter his nuptial chamber with his new bride. According to Callimachus, these were evil omens, all of which pointed to the impending demise of the king of the Huns.

Overcome by the realization that their revered king had left them forever, the Huns fell into a violent frenzy. They tore their clothing, cut off their hair, tortured themselves, and even mutilated their own bodies. This was to show that such a "distinguished warrior might be bewailed," wrote the Gothic historian Jordanes, based on reports by the contemporary Priscus, "not with feminine lamentations and tears, but with manly blood."

After the initial frenzy, the Hunnic shamans, or chief priests, washed and dressed their dead king and laid him out under the huge silken tent. They also surrounded him with his favorite weapons and his imperial regalia. Then they began an elaborate funeral feast attended by hundreds of thousands of Huns and people of associated nations.

In accordance with Hunnic tradition, the funeral feast displayed a mixture of extreme grief and extreme joy. (Based on ancient popular traditions, most Hungarians regard themselves as the direct descendants of the Huns, even though most scholars nowadays reject the idea of a direct link. Whatever the merits of the Hunnic-Hungarian relation, Hungarians still practice the ancient Hunnic custom of "making merry with tears.") But on this occasion the celebrants did so to such a degree that the Gothic monk who witnessed their mourning found it truly amazing. While weeping for their king, the Huns also made merry as if this were a happy event; while celebrating, they also tortured themselves and shed tears of sorrow.

Oh Attila, you mighty
* king of the Huns,*
Died in the Midst
* of your nation,*
Not of an enemy's wounds,
Nor of a friend's treachery,
But amidst happiness and joy,
Without a sense of pain!
Who can view this as death,
When no one can call
* for vengeance?*
—JORDANES
in *The History of the Goths*

Having laid out their dead king, the Huns selected their best horsemen, who surrounded the tent where Attila lay in state. Then they began to gallop around the tent with ever-increasing speed, while at the same time singing funeral dirges. Presently, the chief shaman and his aides placed Attila's remains in three separate coffins. The inner coffin was covered with gold, the second with silver, and the third or outer coffin with iron. This was done in acknowledgment of Attila's greatness as a ruler, as a military leader, and as a conqueror of nations. As put by Jordanes: "These three things suited the mightiest of kings; iron because he subdued the nations, gold and silver because he received the honors of both [Roman] empires."

Before enclosing and sealing Attila into his three caskets, however, the shamans also placed beside him his royal sword, his bow and arrow, his lance, and a multitude of gems and ornaments to demonstrate his unique greatness to the inhabitants of the world beyond. Then they buried him in the dead of night and slew all of the slaves who had prepared his tomb and who had carried out his burial. This was the Huns' way of preventing any living person from ever finding the great king's remains.

A Hunnic diadem, or crown, made of gold and bronze. The symbols of Attila's majesty were buried with him in three coffins: The inner coffin was covered with gold, the second with silver, and the last with iron.

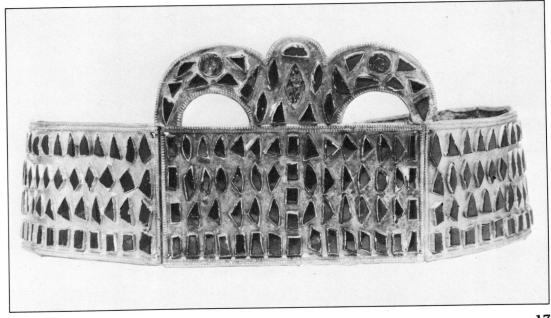

This is the point at which Hungarian national tradition, embodied in several native medieval chronicles, differs significantly from its non-Hungarian counterparts. Hungarian tradition has evolved in the land that used to be the heart of Attila's empire. For this very reason it is more romantic and perhaps also closer to the truth than the version preserved by such Western chroniclers as Priscus, Jordanes, and Callimachus.

According to this native tradition, preserved in Hungarian folklore, Attila's remains were interred under the waters of the Tisza River in central Hungary. The Tisza is a slow, meandering river with multitudes of shifting branches. In Attila's day, the stretch of the river that passed across the Great Hungarian Plain was also filled with numerous constantly shifting islands. Hungarian chroniclers tell us that on the advice of their shamans the Huns decided to inter their beloved king in one of these riverbeds. They did this by building two parallel sandbag dams between one of the islands and the river's shores. Then, once the waters had been removed from this enclosure, they built Attila's tomb deep into the subsoil of the riverbed. It is said that they even widened the bed further by cutting away a section of the island. This work was done quickly and efficiently by using thousands of slaves, all of them to be sacrificed to preserve the secrecy of Attila's final resting place.

Once finished, Attila's casket was carried to his tomb by the very slaves who had prepared it. The procession was led by Attila's sons, his several wives, his generals, and his chief ministers as well as by 14 Germanic, Turkic, and Sarmatian kings who were his vassals. They were accompanied by hundreds of chanting shamans, by tens of thousands of wailing Huns, and by an even greater number of the vassal peoples of Attila's empire, including the Jazyges, the Sarmatians, the Ugros, and the Gepids. All of them joined the Hunnic dignitaries in this funeral procession. Amid unceasing wailing and lamentations the multitude proceeded toward the Tisza River, while the shamans chanted Attila's farewell song to his land and to his people.

The night was dark and the air sweltering as the long procession neared the river, amid the sound of trumpets, drumbeats, and the wailing of thousands. Then all of a sudden the noise stopped, as did the flow of humanity. The funeral procession had reached the point of no return; only those destined to perish could proceed farther. The multitude turned around and began its long journey back to the capital. At the same time the group of slaves that had prepared the tomb and now carried Attila's casket resumed its march toward the river. Only a select group of bowmen remained in place, waiting to put the finishing touches upon this great tragedy.

Soon, the procession of slaves disappeared into the black night, followed by a few of the old shamans, who were to watch over Attila's entombment. They were led by Chief Shaman Káma, already in

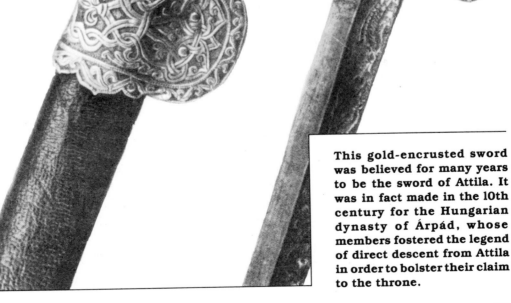

This gold-encrusted sword was believed for many years to be the sword of Attila. It was in fact made in the 10th century for the Hungarian dynasty of Árpád, whose members fostered the legend of direct descent from Attila in order to bolster their claim to the throne.

his eighties and nearly blind. He was the one who had selected Attila's final resting place, who supervised the preparations of his tomb in the bed of the Tisza River, and who was now ready to join his master in the land beyond.

After Attila was laid to rest in his tomb, his magnificent war-horse was sacrificed. The horse's head and hooves were laid next to the king's remains, as were several of the shamans who joined their king voluntarily. Then, at Shaman Káma's order, the slaves began to dismantle the dams, and the waters of the Tisza rushed over the tomb of the great king. Soon, the powerful current of the liberated waters covered and obliterated all signs of Attila's final resting place; the Tisza had reclaimed both its beds. The dimly visible island that divided the two branches of the river appeared to have become smaller and less conspicuous.

Silence descended upon the scene, and a hitherto unfelt fear came to embrace the hearts of Attila's slaves. They seemed to have sensed that the drama was not yet over.

A few minutes later, led by the chief shaman, the slaves began to retrace their steps to Attila's capital. The night was dark and they could barely see the path, but they moved on monotonously, as if under a spell.

After less than an hour they again reached the fork designated as the point of no return. Then the arrows began to fly, shrilly whistling through the darkling sky, landing with a thud as they found their human targets. Shrieks of terror, groans of anguish — the screams of the dying — filled the night air as Attila's bowmen did their job swiftly and efficiently. Within a few minutes, thousands of slaves lay dead or mortally wounded. No one escaped, not even Káma, who chose to sacrifice himself for his king.

The Huns believed that enemies killed in battle and sacrificed slaves would serve the dead hero in the world beyond. Thus, Attila, king of the Huns, Scourge of God, ruler of the great Hunnic Empire, passed into history, assured that he would be accompanied by men willing and able to serve him.

I have always fought under
  the shadow of Death,
I have always challenged
  him openly,
Yet Death was never able
  to get the best of me.
But now He had ambushed
  me treacherously,
Ending my life and my dreams,
At the very moment when
  I was enjoying
The embraces of my
  beautiful bride.
      —GEZA GARDONYI
Attila's death song from the
novel *The Invisible Man*

Western traditions differ from the Hungarian version only insofar as they know nothing about Attila's alleged underwater grave. They also cite his secret funeral and the massacre that followed it. These sources, however, speak of a funeral on the Hungarian steppes somewhere in the vicinity of Attila's capital. But since not even the site of the former capital is known, no one can even guess the location of the grave.

The Tisza is still there, but its meandering waters have shifted many times over into ever-newer channels. Most of its islands have disappeared, and many of its branches have turned into backwaters and dead channels. Others have dried up completely, with no sign that at one time there used to be a river there. Attila's grave is still intact; it has eluded discovery, and for this reason it has fired the imagination for generations.

But although Attila's final resting place is unknown, his name is recognized throughout the world. To the Hungarians, Turks, and various other Turkic peoples in the Near East and central Asia, his name symbolizes heroism, courage, and greatness. To these nations the Age of Attila represents one of the high points of their history. But to the Western mind, Attila's name stands for barbarism, terror, conquest, and destruction. Which is the real Attila?

A rock carving from southern Siberia shows scenes of Hunnic life in the 2nd and 3rd centuries. At left, an ox pulls a sled; at right, two riders take part in what is thought to be a religious ceremony; the figure in the center stirs the contents of a sacred vessel.

2

The World of the Huns

As is the case with virtually all of Attila's early life, the exact year of his birth is unknown. It is believed that he was born in the final years of the 4th century, probably in A.D. 400. He was the son of Mundzuk, the deceased elder brother of King Ruga, who had ruled Hunnia before Attila. It is also known that at one time in his youth Attila had been a political hostage in the Western Roman Empire. Being the nephew of King Ruga, he was exchanged for a prominent Roman to ensure peace between the two empires.

The name of the Roman hostage was Flavius Aëtius, who stayed for years in the Hunnic Empire and became very knowledgeable about Hunnic life, culture, and fighting methods. Aëtius learned to respect the Huns, and later he would often rely on Hunnic auxiliaries in his struggle to keep the sinking Western Roman Empire afloat. Yet toward the end of his life he became Attila's number one opponent and nemesis. Attila was even forced to fight his greatest and least-successful battle against this undoubtedly worthy Roman.

On the Caspian Sea, there appeared the Huns, horsemen belonging to a barbarian race unknown till then. These plunderers were the forerunners of the catastrophe destined to fall on the Roman world and to shatter it to pieces beyond the possibility of recovery.
—FERDINAND LOT
French historian

A gold fibula, or clasp, made by the Ostrogoths, a Germanic people. In the mid-370s, the Huns invaded eastern Europe and quickly overwhelmed the Ostrogoths. This was the first of the Huns' European conquests.

Attila the Hun appeared on the stage of history in the early 430s, just as unexpectedly as the Huns themselves had some six decades earlier. He came to be known to the world only upon assuming the leadership of his people in 434. By that time, however, he was already in his mid-thirties and ready to pursue what he believed to be his divinely ordained destiny to build a new world empire. He was encouraged in this goal by several signs, including the unexpected appearance of a sacred sword, the so-called Sword of God.

The Huns had appeared in the eastern part of Europe, in what is today the Soviet Union, in the last 30 years of the 4th century. They had crossed the Volga River in the mid-370s and then immediately attacked and destroyed the kingdom of the Ostrogoths, a Germanic people who a century and a half earlier had moved from their northwestern homelands to eastern Europe. The Hunnic defeat of the Ostrogoths was followed by their subjugation or dislodgment of many other related tribes, including the Herulians, Scirians, and Rugians as well as the powerful Germanic Visigoths.

Having conquered much of eastern Europe within about two decades, in the 390s the Huns moved into central Europe and began to penetrate the provinces of the Eastern Roman (Byzantine) Empire. Led by

A band of Hsiung-nu, or Eastern Huns, depicted in a detail from a 14th-century Chinese silk scroll. The scroll tells the story of the Huns' abduction of Lady Wen-chi from her father's house in Shensi province in A.D. 196; she was held for 12 years and then ransomed.

one of their regional kings, Uldin, they conquered much of Pannonia in the region of present-day Hungary. There they subjugated other Germanic and Iranian tribes, such as the Vandals, Quadi, Silingals, Gepids, and Alans. Many of the dislodged tribes moved on, and on December 31, 406, for the first time in history, the barbarians crossed the Rhine River into the territories of the Western Roman Empire, where they clashed with the German Burgundians.

During the next decades, while Attila was growing into manhood and preparing to assume the leadership of Hunnia, the Huns pursued their conquests relentlessly. They led several successful wars against the Persian Empire in the Near East. They consolidated their rule over many Germanic, Slavic, Turkic, and Iranian tribes in central and eastern Europe. They conquered the Caucasus region that separates Europe from the Middle East. And they also extended their sway into their ancestral homeland, central Asia. At the same time, they became involved in the internal affairs of the two Roman empires, both as conquerors and as allies.

Under King Ruga, the Huns transferred the seat of their empire to the center of present-day Hungary, where they planted the seeds of their traditions, some of which survived right up to today.

And against these horsemen the Ostrogoths could only place their spear-wielding footmen, who proved just so many targets for arrows. The Huns simply rolled over them, hardly knowing anything was in the way, and the Ostrogoth kingdom vanished in a day.
—ISAAC ASIMOV
from *The Dark Ages*

Thus, only a half century after appearing on the eastern frontiers of Europe, the Huns made themselves a critical factor in European politics, even to the point of endangering the very existence of the two Roman empires. By dislodging the Germanic tribes from their eastern and central European homelands, they began what are known as the barbarian invasions. This mass movement of nations undermined both Roman empires and ultimately led to the fall of Rome itself only a few years after Attila's death. The Huns, therefore, were indirectly responsible for the rise of feudal Europe.

The unexpected appearance and rapid successes of the Huns puzzled the contemporary world. Christian writers immediately attributed all sorts of strange characteristics to them, often describing them in less-than-human terms. Like Genghis Khan's Mongols some eight centuries later, the Huns at the time of their appearance were thought to be God's curse upon the Christian world for having strayed from the true path of Christianity.

The origins of the Huns are lost in the mist of time. Although today much more is known about them than ever before, there are still many blank spots in their history. Moreover, historians' descriptions of the period do not match the portrait preserved in the romantic legends of medieval Hungarian chroniclers.

These Hungarian legends all accept the belief that there was a close relationship between the Huns and the Hungarians (or Magyars, as Hungarians call themselves) of today. For example, *The Legend of the White Stag*, which is one of the most oft-quoted epics on the origins of the Magyar people, holds that the Huns and the Hungarians are sister nations who descended from two brothers.

Named Hunor and Magor (hence the word Magyar), the brothers were the sons of the biblical king Nimrod and his wife Eneh. King Nimrod and his nation lived somewhere in the east beyond unspecified mountains. Both father and sons were mighty warriors and magnificent hunters. Day after day they would go out to hunt far and wide across their realm.

It so happened that one day Hunor and Magor were out hunting in the company of their 200 retainers. Suddenly and quite unexpectedly, a beautiful white stag appeared in front of them. They immediately began a chase that took them to a new country and ultimately to the foundation of two new nations, the Huns and the Hungarians. As described in one version of this heroic legend, which appeared recently in English in this author's translation:

A detail from the so-called Viennese Illuminated Chronicle, a 14th-century Hungarian manuscript, depicting the legend of the white stag. According to the legend, Hunor and Magor, the sons of a biblical king, chased a white stag until it led them to the land where they founded the Hungarian nation.

They [Hunor and Magor] followed the stag up hills and down hills, across wide plains and meandering rivers, from early morning until sunset. . . . At dusk the stag vanished, [but] next morning . . . [it] was there again, as if waiting for the chase to begin. Hunor and Magor could not resist. They followed him once more across deep valleys, high mountains, bottomless marshes, and nightmarish swamps into hitherto unseen and unexplored lands. And this was repeated day after day. Thus the wondrous stag lured the sons of Nimrod further and further away from their father's kingdom. . . . Finally, on the seventh day, they reached a land so wondrous that it outshone all others. . . . It turned out to be the land of Meotis on the borders of Persia . . . [where] the white stag disappeared and the tired hunters bedded down for the night.

In the middle of the night they awoke to enchanting music. They soon discovered that the wondrous stag had lured them to the hiding place of the lovely daughters of King Dúl . . . and their two-hundred ladies-in-waiting. . . . The brothers immediately fell in love with the

The Great Wall of China at the Nan-k'ou Pass. In order to defend themselves against the fierce Asiatic Huns, the Chinese emperors built defensive ramparts that ultimately stretched 1,600 miles. Some 300,000 workers, most of them convicted criminals, took part in the construction.

two princesses and took them as their wives. Each of their warriors took a wife from among the other maidens. After this . . . they settled down, prospered, and grew in numbers and in power. It was thus that Hunor and Magor and their two-hundred warriors became the progenitors of two great sister nations, the Huns and the Magyars, also called Hungarians.

This is how the romantic traditions of the Hungarians see the origin of the Huns. The truth is somewhat less romantic and more in line with the general history of the equestrian peoples (horse-riding nomads) of the great plains of eastern Europe and Asia. It is known, for example, that the Huns were only one of many Turkic peoples of central Asia who from time to time rode out from their original homeland to start on a path of conquest and create large equestrian empires.

The first of these Turkic empires was established by the Eastern Huns, known as Hiung-nu or Hsiung-nu, in the 3rd century B.C. In those days the Hunnic tribes north of China were united by an able leader into a tribal federation. This federation soon became a major rival to the Chinese Empire that was just being consolidated by the Ch'in dynasty (which gave its name to China).

Indirectly, these Asiatic Huns were also responsible for the Great Wall of China. In the decade and a half between 221 B.C. and 206 B.C., their constant attacks against the Chinese Empire forced the Ch'in emperors to connect many local defensive walls into a continuous rampart that ultimately stretched over 1,600 miles. During the next 150 years, this wall was further extended and strengthened by the Han dynasty, which was forced to continue the struggle against the Hiung-nu.

The Asiatic Huns reached the climax of their power in the early 2nd century B.C. Under the Great Khan Mao-tun, their empire stretched from the Aral Sea in west-central Asia all the way to the Korean peninsula in the east. As such, the territory under Hunnic rule was wider than the United States today, even though the western Hunnic tribes were only loosely associated with it.

The Hiung-nu Empire, however, did not last very long. Already toward the end of the 2nd century B.C. it was under increasing Chinese pressure. This military pressure gradually eroded Hunnic power, and eventually the last independent Hun ruler, Emperor Hu-han-sie, was forced to accept Chinese overlordship in 52 B.C. The Huns fell apart into scores of small tribal nations that were unable to reassert themselves for about four centuries.

The new dawn of Hunnic power came in the 4th century A.D. Led by a military genius whose name is given in Hungarian chronicles as Balambér, some of the Hunnic tribes of central Asia were able to coalesce once more into a strong tribal federation. Then, moving through the gap between the Ural Mountains and the Caspian Sea, they began their push into the steppes of eastern Europe, finally crossing the Volga River in A.D. 372.

For several thousand years the homeland of the Turkic Huns and the scene of their rising and falling equestrian empires was the Great Eurasian Plain. This vast flatland of steppes, plateaus, grasslands, and semideserts stretches over 5,000 miles from the western Soviet Union across central Asia to the Sea of Okhotsk at the eastern end of the Asian continent.

For thousands of years the ancestors of the Huns led a seminomadic life on this vast land. They hunted, fished, and raised horses, cattle, and sheep. Their animals served as the main source of their food (meat, milk, cheese). They were also important in making clothing (leather garments, felt, shoes); tools (kitchen implements, needles, yarns); dwellings (tents, wooden houses); and even weapons (knife handles, arrowheads, bow and arrow parts). Because they relied so much on their animals, the Huns had extremely large herds, which were in constant need of food and water. Therefore, it was only natural for them to move from place to place, or as the Chinese sources put it, "to follow water and grass." But these were not haphazard wanderings. Rather, they were seasonal movements between their winter quarters and summer pastures.

They are ignorant of the use of the plow and of fixed habitations, whether houses or huts. Being perpetually nomadic, they are inured from childhood to cold, hunger, and thirst.
—AMMIANUS MARCELLINUS
Roman soldier
and historian

Although seminomadic, the Huns also practiced some agriculture. They raised grain, ate various types of bread and cereal, and used fibers to make linen fabrics. At the same time they also spun wool and made woolen textiles.

They were extremely good artisans. They made bows and arrows of unmatched quality, excellent sabers, lances, and lassos, and complex and many-layered armors, shields, and helmets as well as sturdy saddles and harnesses. They also made leather clothing, shoes, various personal and household implements (vessels, mirrors, caldrons), and even exquisite jewelry. The latter included rings, earrings, decorative masks, and crowns. The artisans also made heavily decorated saber hilts, scabbards, and quivers for the Hunnic nobility.

The Huns' primary abode was the yurt, which was a large tentlike structure made of wooden frames and covered by felt. Their yurts were huge by contemporary European standards. Moreover, they were also comfortable, spacious, airy, and clean. And what was equally important for people who usu-

This scene from a Chinese silk scroll shows an encampment of Asiatic Huns. The tentlike structures in the center and the left foreground are yurts. The Huns' principal means of shelter, yurts were easily assembled and disassembled, making them ideal dwellings for nomadic peoples.

31

ally moved with the seasons, these yurts were also easily disassembled and reassembled as needed.

By the time the Huns had reached the forests of Europe in the 5th century, they also built large and complex wooden houses and even wooden palaces for their military aristocracy. This is best exemplified by Attila's own capital on the Hungarian Plain, which the Hungarian chroniclers call Budavár after Attila's brother Buda, or Bléda, while the German epic Song of the Nibelungs records it as Etzelburg, after Etzel, the German name for Attila. Not identical to medieval Buda (now part of Budapest) nor even situated on the same site, this city impressed even the learned Greek envoy, Priscus.

The partial switch from yurts to wooden houses by Attila's Huns may have been the result of Gothic-Germanic influence upon Hunnic society, for Attila's empire included most of the prominent German tribes of those days. Yet it was also a natural outgrowth of the Huns' long-standing yurt architecture, which involved the use of extensive woodworking. And it certainly reflected their unwillingness to live in masonry houses; like other peoples who lived close to nature, the Huns loathed being confined to the interior of stone or brick buildings.

Hunnic society was patriarchal and hierarchical. The Huns believed that qualities of leadership were inheritable and that these were passed on from father to son. Members of the nobility were believed to be in possession of unique leadership qualities, and if they excelled beyond expectations, they joined the special rank of heroes. If commoners excelled, on the other hand, they were elevated into the ranks of the nobility and thus began a new noble dynasty.

The members of the nobility had great influence in political matters. Although the king had absolute control over the masses, he was not an absolute ruler. He had to share his powers with the Hunnic nobility. All major decisions were made in the grand council, composed of the Hunnic nobility and leaders of the associated nations.

Below the nobles were the common Huns and

then the servant or slave classes. Although they owned slaves, the Huns, contrary to more sedentary societies, did not believe in hereditary slavery. For this reason, slaves were often freed, ransomed, or simply married into the family.

The hierarchical structure of Hunnic society also extended into the family. The Huns lived in extended families, where all forms of contact and all relationships were strictly controlled by traditional etiquette. Every member of the family had a designated place in the yurt and had to eat and sleep according to the socially determined hierarchical order. The place of honor was always occupied by the head of the family, and the places to his immediate right and left were reserved for those next in honor.

Like all seminomadic and equestrian societies in those days, the Huns also practiced polygamy. In theory the adult male Hun could have as many wives as he wished. In practice, however, having more than one wife was the prerogative only of the powerful and the wealthy. A prospective wife always had to be purchased from her father, and the price of even an ordinary young woman was very high. The daughter of a distinguished family, on the other hand, cost a fortune. Because of this, most Huns were forced to live in monogamy.

In the households of polygamous husbands, the hierarchical structure of Hunnic society also intruded into the relationship between the various wives. The first wife always occupied a special legal place in Hunnic society. Thus, irrespective of her momentary relationship to her husband, she always remained the chief wife and overseer of the family. All other wives were placed under her direction, and they were hardly more than concubines. At the same time, most prominent men who could afford to do so established separate households for their various wives. Even so, only the first wife's sons were deemed to be fully legitimate and the inheritors of their father's leadership abilities and position.

As an example of this practice, Attila's first wife, Arykan (a name meaning "pure princess"), had her very own court, hosted Byzantine ambassadors, and presided over sizable estates within the Hunnic Empire. Known as Ríka or Réka in Hungarian heroic legends, she was fully assured in her position, knowing well that only her three sons had the right of succession to the throne.

As a result of this system, women were highly prized and well treated in Hunnic society. They had a good deal of independence, were relatively unrestricted in their activities, and could not be made destitute by the temporary emotional involvements of their husbands. Their independence was further augmented by the mobility of Hunnic society and by the fact that their husbands were often away on long military campaigns. As a result, they often had to perform tasks that in other societies were usually reserved for men. Thus, like their husbands they were excellent equestrians, and they could also handle weapons effectively. Consequently, they were neither defenseless nor unrespected. They were certainly held in greater honor than their sisters in the two Roman empires.

The single most important animal in Hunnic society was the horse, upon which depended the success of their whole civilization. Although generally described as short, shaggy, snub nosed, and ugly, these Asiatic horses were hardy creatures indeed. They were accustomed to all sorts of hardships, including extreme cold and hot weather, from which they did not even need shelter. Without horses and the resulting cavalry attacks, the Huns would never have been able to conquer powerful states and build their own far-reaching empires. Several contemporary observers went so far as to claim that the Huns were born on horseback; spent much of their lives on horseback; fought, conquered, and negotiated on horseback; and even died on horseback. Some of this is substantiated by the Roman historian Ammianus, who described the Huns as being "almost glued to their horses." Ammianus also claimed that they "performed [even] their ordinary tasks [on horseback]."

The quality of Hunnic horsemanship is also attested to by the claim that children of the Huns began to ride before they could walk. As observed by the contemporary scribe Apollinaris Sidonius, "scarce had the infant learnt to stand without his mother's aid when a horse takes him on his back." Naturally, these children soon became unparalleled horsemen, and their skills were the envy of most of their contemporaries. Certainly all written sources agree that the sons and daughters of no other nation could equal the Huns in horsemanship.

If horses were the Huns' war machines, then the reflexed composite bow was their most terrifying weapon. This dreaded weapon was a Turkic invention and originated in central Asia. It was used by most of the horse-riding nomads from that region, and it was feared by all their adversaries. The Hunnic bow could hurl an arrow as far as 1,500 feet, although its effective range extended only up to 600 feet (still a considerable distance). The reflexed bow's unparalleled power rested on the fact that when unstrung it reversed its position. Thus it packed a powerful punch, and it was able to withstand the immense stresses stemming from its reflexed shape and reversed stringing simply because of its laminated construction. The construction of such a bow used a combination of special types of wood, sinew, and horn as well as a drawn-out seasoning process that lasted from 5 to 10 years under the care of expert craftsmen. Consequently, a warrior's bow was very valuable, and it probably was the most highly prized possession of an average Hunnic family.

Almost equal in importance were the Huns' fighting methods, which relied very heavily on the use of the bow and arrow. Being extremely skilled horsemen and bowmen, the Huns were able to release volleys of arrows in any direction while in full gallop. They could do this either during frontal attack or in the course of feigned or real flight. Feigned flight, which meant giving the impression of defeat so as to disorganize the pursuing enemy's military formations, was one of the Huns' most commonly used deceptive strategies.

Their effective use of the reflexed bow would not have been possible without the use of another Turkic invention, the stirrup. This ingenious cen-

A silver plate from the Ural Mountains shows a mounted hunter using stirrups. The stirrup was an Asiatic invention: It allowed Hunnic horsemen to stand in the saddle and use both hands to draw their powerful bows, even while riding at a full gallop.

tral Asiatic contraption, unknown in the West at that time, permitted the Hunnic bowmen to stand up in the saddle and to handle their bows and arrows with both hands even while in full gallop. The stirrup was likewise useful in hand-to-hand combat, for it permitted the Huns to handle simultaneously their sabers and shields, their lances and shields, their shields and lassos, or their lassos and sabers.

The Huns' religion can be called nature worship. They believed in the existence of a wide variety of gods and spirits who controlled human destinies. They also held that there were specially chosen

Soothsayers examine the intestines of a bull in order to foretell the future. Soothsaying was a common practice in the ancient world; military commanders were reluctant to enter into battle without first receiving a favorable omen.

persons who had the power to communicate with the spiritual world. These were their shamans, or priests, who occupied a high place in Hunnic society.

The shamans were in constant contact with their gods and spirits, but they also served as medical doctors and oracles. Hunnic kings and military leaders would never undertake anything without consulting these seers for advice. And the shamans did give advice through a series of rituals involving animal sacrifice and the examination of the internal organs and bones of these animals for omens of good or bad luck.

During Attila's time in the mid-5th century, a number of Huns converted to Christianity. This was partially the result of their increased contact with the Christian world and partially of the Huns' well-known tolerance for all religions. The Christianity of the Hunnic converts, however, was Arianism, which did not recognize Jesus on par with God the Father as did mainstream Christianity. For this reason it was later proclaimed a heresy. Hunnic converts opted for Arianism simply because most of their subject Germanic tribes were also Arian Christians. Moreover, Attila preferred this strain of Christianity for his subjects, precisely because it divided them from the faith of the inhabitants of the two Roman empires.

Like the Romans, the Huns also believed in the divine nature of kingship. The Romans routinely called their emperors gods simply because of these rulers' exalted positions. In the case of the Huns, however, this belief was an outgrowth of their ancestor worship and their tendency to attribute unique powers to direct descendants of their great national heroes. For example, they were fully convinced of Attila's divinely ordained destiny. This belief was further strengthened during Attila's reign by various miraculous happenings, some of which have been preserved in Hungarian chronicles. For these reasons the Huns looked upon Attila with considerable awe and regarded him the same way as did the Persians their King of Kings and the Chinese their Son of Heaven.

uidelicet tene ptis que
temanserant Cathalaun
ie parmint. Cumaq

3

The Birth of a World Conqueror

According to the calculations of the Christian priests who lived in the lands of the setting sun, the year was A.D. 400. These shamans of Christianity, who said they believed in only a single god, had the strange custom of counting the passage of time from the birth of their prophet — whom they also called God. It was even stranger that the prophet-god of these Christians was later crucified. Yet, they continued to pray to him.

To the Huns this made no sense. How could these dwellers of stifling cities where all free men of the steppes would suffocate within the span of a few days believe in a god who had permitted himself to be nailed to a wooden cross? Was it not more logical to believe that the affairs of the world were neatly divided among several divinities, each of whom had his or her sphere of influence? Was it not more praiseworthy to place the mighty Hadúr, the god of war, at the head of all gods, as did the glorious Hunnic nation from time immemorial?

Below average height when afoot, the Hun is great when mounted on his steed.
—APOLLINARIS SIDONIUS
Roman prelate and writer

Attila with a sword and shield, in a detail from the Viennese Illuminated Chronicle. On the shield is a representation of the *turul*, a mythical bird adopted as the symbol of the Árpád dynasty. According to legend, both Árpád's father and Attila himself were born of the union between a woman and a turul.

A clay carving of the head of a Scythian, taken from a burial mound in Transcaucasia, in southern Russia. The Huns conquered this region in the late 4th century; it formed part of the empire that Attila inherited from his grandfather Khan Balambér and father, King Mundzuk.

So thought Khan Balambér, who now rode along the shores of the mighty Atil River (known in Russian as the Volga) on the vast plains that he and his nation had conquered nearly three decades before. Balambér loved this river and the immense steppes that enfolded it for hundreds of miles in three directions: toward the rising sun, where the steppes crossed right through Turkestan, the ancient homeland of his nation; toward the upper course of the river, where the grasslands rolled into the frigid tundras of the misty north; and toward the setting sun, where these same prairies melted into the mountains inhabited by the Christians.

While Balambér rested his gaze upon this vast land, his mind went back to his early childhood and youth in central Asia. He recalled his rise to manhood, his encounters with the beautiful women of Hunnia, and his impressive triumphs in war. His mind also returned to that glorious year some 28 summers ago when at the head of his nation he first beheld the magnificent Atil. He fell in love with the great river right then and there and decided to establish the new center of his empire at the very spot where he stood, where the river made a great bend, only to resume its march to the Caspian Sea. Now, nearly three decades later, Khan Balambér stood once more at the same spot, beholding the Father of All Waters as he did many years ago. It was the very place where he had dreamed his dreams as the young leader of his people, and it was also the place where he wished to join Mother Earth now that he had grown old and frail.

Balambér left his capital just before dawn. He rode out on his faithful war-horse to rest his gaze once more upon the great river. Only a day earlier he had still been uncertain of his nation's future. But then something happened that restored his hope — the birth of Mundzuk's son. It was the same child whose glorious destiny had been foretold many generations earlier by some of the greatest oracles of his nation.

Mundzuk was Balambér's favorite son and his personal choice to follow him on the throne. True, Balambér still had a surviving brother, Karaton, who could claim a share of royal power. But Karaton was old himself, and he was not expected to survive Balambér by very long.

Fate, however, would have it another way. Soon after being selected by his father as his favored successor, Mundzuk fell gravely ill. According to the shamans, he was not expected to live much longer than his father. Khan Balambér also had three other sons, but for reasons unknown to him none of them carried the spark of leadership, as did the unfortunate Mundzuk. Having learned of Mundzuk's illness, Balambér became despondent. He waited for a miracle to occur.

It came with the birth of a grandson. This child, so said the ancient prophecy, would raise the Hunnic nation to heights never before attained. He would become the new founding father of his nation, and the size of his empire would exceed all previous empires the world had ever known.

Somewhere in Balambér's mind, a connection was drawn between his young grandson and the mighty river before him. There in front of the conqueror Balambér flowed the Father of All Waters, and there in one of his yurts lay the future father of his regenerated nation. Therefore, let his grandson be named after this river; let him be called Atil (Father), or even better, Attila (Little Father), that he may be reminded of his destiny every time he hears his name.

And so, in the early spring of the year 400, Attila, the future world conqueror and acknowledged Scourge of God, began his earthly journey at the very moment when his grandfather was preparing to end his own.

Only a few days after Attila's birth, Khan Balambér joined his ancestors in the land beyond. He was buried on a low hill next to the river Atil, at a spot close to the river's bend that he himself had selected. Attila was too young to know this, or even to remember Khan Balambér. Yet, throughout his youth, he always felt very close to his deceased grandfather. He felt much closer to him than to any other of his 32 illustrious ancestors, whose genealogical line stretched back 7 centuries. And this feeling of closeness to Khan Balambér became even

Asiatic horsemen shoot arrows at a flock of birds. The reflexed bows used by the Huns were powerful enough to propel an arrow 1,500 feet. Hunnic women were often as skilled in riding and hunting as were the men.

more intense in Attila after the death of his own father, King Mundzuk.

After Balambér's passing, political power over Hunnia came to be divided among his brother, Khan Karaton, and Balambér's four sons. In addition to the very sick Mundzuk, there were Oktar, Ruga, and Aybars. The elderly Karaton remained in the region between the Volga and the Don to oversee the eastern half of the empire. His nephews, on the other hand, continued their relentless push to the west. Attila's early years, therefore, were spent in constant warfare and periodic resettlement as his father's and his uncle's armies subdued one nation after another. By his early teens, the Hunnic armies had already penetrated the Carpathian Basin, and Attila probably grew to manhood in the region of present-day Hungary.

Although his uncles visibly disliked Attila, he had nothing to fear from them — nothing to fear, that is, until his father's death, which occurred just a few years after Balambér's. Attila, therefore, became an orphan long before he was ready to face the world alone.

Following King Mundzuk's death Attila came under the control of his three uncles, who made his life difficult. They probably would have had him killed had the shamans not watched over the boy. Yet, with a mixture of awe and envy, they all were forced to watch him grow in stature and wisdom. Attila survived his uncles' envy, but not without some pain and anger.

The protection of the powerful shamans assured not only Attila's survival and well-being but his training and education for the leadership of his nation. He learned to ride a horse before he could walk, was instructed in the use of the bow and arrow before he was three and the saber before he was five. Attila thus became an expert horseman, marksman, and swordsman even before he had reached his teens.

During the same period, Attila also became an excellent military tactician. Under the careful eye of Chief Shaman Káma, he would organize the boys of his clan into small regiments. Then he would train

---

Like a hunter who studies the paths in the jungle, so [did Attila study] the shortcomings of the Roman society, the weaknesses of the Roman people . . . the incompetence of the emperors, the corruption of their statesmen, the absence of morality among their masses; everything that could be helpful to him later, and could serve as inspiration for his boldness and genius.

—AMEDÉE THIERRY
19th-century
French historian

44

them, conduct military exercises with them, and lead them into mock battles. While training Attila in the art of war and military leadership, his tutors also made certain that their young charge would also be ready for peace and diplomacy.

By Attila's time the Hunnic Empire embraced several nationalities and many scores of tribes. These included numerous related Turkic tribes and at least an equal number of unrelated Germanic and Slavic peoples. This huge empire stretched over much of eastern Europe and central Asia. The Huns ruled this empire, and for this reason Hunnic was its primary language. But Gothic (early German) also became a commonly spoken language. Thus, while most of the subject peoples of the empire picked up Hunnic as a second language, Hunnic tribal and military leaders tended to learn Gothic, too.

A Byzantine mosaic shows the Roman emperor Constantine the Great (306—37) holding the city of Constantinople, the capital of the Eastern Roman Empire. Constantine was among the last effective Roman emperors.

Attila was no different. We know that he grew up speaking both Hunnic and Gothic. Moreover, before reaching adulthood he also learned Latin and Greek. The last two were the official languages of the Western and Eastern Roman empires, and his stay there as a hostage forced him to learn both of these classical tongues. Attila may also have known some Slavic, but this is not certain; the Slavs were numerous among the Hunnic subjects, but unlike the Germans they never really played a significant role in the leadership of Hunnia.

While studying the art of war and the languages of his future subjects, Attila also became deeply immersed in the study of the history of his nation and his ancestors. He would ask the best Hunnic minstrels to recite to him the heroic deeds of his forefathers. And he would also ask them to relate everything they knew of the history of such competing empires as those of the Romans and the Persians. Whenever possible, he would quiz the ambassadors of those nations about their nations' history. He would carefully note all details and then recite these to himself time and time again. Knowledge, he knew, was power.

Attila's relatively peaceful life took a sudden and unexpected turn soon after his father's death, when Flavius Aëtius, the son of a prominent Roman general, appeared in King Ruga's court. Aëtius had been sent by the Roman Empire to the Hunnic court as a hostage to assure the Huns of the Romans' good faith. He stayed for a number of years, learning the Hunnic language and becoming thoroughly familiar with the way the Huns lived — and how they fought. All this would help him later when he would have to face the Huns on the battlefield. But this knowledge would also aid Aëtius in securing Hunnic help for the preservation of the Roman Empire and would help him to survive in the midst of the court intrigue that plagued the Western Roman Empire during the last century of its existence.

Aëtius was a few years older than Attila, yet the two boys became good friends. While Aëtius learned from Attila about Hunnic society and the Hunnic ruling class, Attila learned from Aëtius about the

Roman world. Thus, when a few years later Attila was dispatched by his uncle as a hostage to the Roman court at Ravenna, he was well prepared to face the court intrigues.

According to the 19th-century French historian Amedée Thierry:

> Aëtius first learned about military tactics among the Huns, while Attila did so among the Romans. Like a hunter who studies the paths in the jungle, so [did Attila study] the short-comings of [Roman] society, the weaknesses of the Roman people . . . the incompetence of their emperors, the corruption of their states-men, the absence of morality among their masses; in other words, everything that could in any way be helpful to him later, and could serve as inspiration for his boldness and his genius.
>
> Attila and Aëtius were bound together by a strange friendship, which revealed itself in the exchange of small gifts and services. [Later] the Roman would supply the Hun with Latin sec-retaries and interpreters, while the Hun would send the Roman unique gifts, including amus-ing artifacts and once even a midget.
>
> These two men respected each other, and secretly even feared each other. They were like two rivals, who knew that perhaps one day they would have to face one another on the battle-field. They also believed only they were worthy to measure each other's strength.

It is uncertain how long Aëtius stayed at the Hunnic court, but it must have been several years, for he became completely fluent in Hunnic and also very knowledgeable about the Hunnic way of life. Attila was sent off as a hostage to the Western Ro-man court a year or two after Aëtius's arrival. This was probably done on the basis of an earlier ar-rangement that involved the simultaneous ex-change of the two boys.

At the time of this exchange the Roman Empire was only a shadow of its former self. It had been cut into two parts, and the old Roman virtues that had built this huge empire had all but disappeared. Its formerly efficient administrative and military sys-tems had degenerated into complex and unworkable

Roman soldiers defend a fort against attacking barbarians. As the leadership and fighting spirit of the Romans declined, they were repeatedly attacked by the Huns and other tribes; often, they could only secure peace by paying tribute money.

bureaucracies, and both halves were headed by incompetent rulers. The reforms of some of the more able emperors such as Diocletian (284–305) and Constantine the Great (306–37) did put a temporary stop to this decay. In the long run, however, not even they could stop the disintegration of the Western Empire, which had even transferred its seat from Rome to Milan in 285 and then to Ravenna in 423.

The empire's problems were further increased by a series of barbarian invasions; the Visigoths, Ostrogoths, Vandals, Burgundians, and other Germanic tribes, dislodged from their homelands by the Huns, were harrying the imperial borders. Now flabby and inefficient, the empire was unable to defend itself. The two alternatives left were to either pay off the invaders or play them off against each other. And both methods were used, in Milan and Ravenna as well as in the eastern capital, Constantinople. The two emperors often paid tributes to various barbarian rulers to buy peace. At the same time, they often enlisted these leaders into imperial service and used them against each other.

Through these policies the Eastern Roman Empire was ultimately able to save and reconstitute itself into the so-called Byzantine Empire, which lasted for another thousand years. The Western Roman Empire, however, was unable to do so. By the 5th century it had become the playground of crude barbarian kings and corrupt Roman emperors.

In the first quarter of the 5th century, when Attila was dispatched as a hostage, the ruler of the Western Roman Empire was Honorius (395–423). He was both corrupt and incompetent and fell under the influence of a Vandal mercenary named Stilicho. Stilicho soon named himself commander in chief of the Roman armies and became the emperor's father-in-law as well.

Honorius, threatened, had Stilicho murdered, but it only worsened his predicament. The Visigoths, sensing an opening, attacked the empire. Led by King Alaric, they conquered much of Italy, sacking Rome itself in 410 and establishing themselves in Gaul (known today as France) soon thereafter. At the same time, the Vandals moved into Spain and by the 430s succeeded in wresting all of North Africa from the Roman Empire.

The situation was hardly better in the Eastern Roman Empire, except that its capital, Constantinople, proved to be more defensible than Rome. Ruled by the weak and incompetent Theodosius II (408–50), it too began a slide downward. Theodosius permitted his scheming sister, Pulcheria, to run the affairs of his empire while he devoted himself to self-gratification. Given these realities, the

Yet this absolute ruler had little idea of government beyond conquest, slave-hunting, and looting.
—C. W. PREVITE-ORTON
English historian, on Attila

Stilicho, a Vandal merce-
nary, gained great influence
over Emperor Honorius and
was appointed commander in
chief of the Roman armies.
Honorius later had Stilicho
murdered, and this deed inspired the barbarian tribes to
attack Rome.

future looked bleak for both Roman empires even
before Attila's rise to the leadership of Hunnia.

Attila was elated by what he saw during his several
years as a hostage in the Western Empire, for he
concluded that the empire was ready to fall to the
first serious rival. The Romans, he believed, were
morally weak and corrupt; he would never follow the
example of the Vandal Stilicho or the Visigoth Alaric
and give up his way of life for the pleasures of Roman
society. Attila vowed never to give up the old ways

nor to permit his nation to do so. He kept to this promise throughout his life, and for this reason he always lived a simple, Spartan existence, even during the height of his power. This is clearly evident from a description of Attila, offered by the learned Greek envoy Priscus, at the banquet he gave in honor of the Eastern Roman embassy in the year 449. The Attila depicted by Priscus in this eyewitness account is a far cry from the unrestrained barbarian usually portrayed in most Western writings.

In his late teens, Attila became certain that one day he would return to Italy not as a hostage but as a conqueror. His faith was based on his belief in his own unique destiny and on his conviction that fate had singled him out to create a new world upon the ruins of the old. And once back in Hunnia, he went to work systematically to prepare himself and his nation for the fulfillment of that destiny.

> *His dress was plain, having care for nothing other than to be clean, nor was the sword by his side, nor the clasps of his barbarian boots, nor the bridle of his horse, like those of other Scythians [Huns], adorned with gold or gems or anything of high price.*
> —PRISCUS
> Byzantine chronicler

4

The Dual Kingship

It was the 26th year of Emperor Theodosius II's reign, marked in the Christian calendar as A.D. 434. The barbarian Huns were again on the move, preparing to ravage the Balkan territories of Theodosius's empire — although it might more properly have been called Pulcheria's empire, for she, instead of her weak brother, was actually running the affairs of state.

At this desperate hour Theodosius — who, as ruler of the Eastern Roman Empire, was also viewed as the head of the true Orthodox Christian faith — beseeched God for a miracle of deliverance. As related in an account written in about 439 by the church historian Socrates Scholasticus, Emperor Theodosius "speedily obtained what he sought, for the chief of the barbarians, whose name was Rugas [Ruga], was struck by a thunderbolt." Then, continued Socrates, "a plague followed which destroyed most of the men who were under him, and . . . fire came down from heaven, and consumed many of the survivors." If we can believe Socrates Scholasticus, this means that at the moment of the impending Hunnic invasion, King Ruga was suddenly and unexpectedly killed by some accident of nature, and at the same time his army was decimated by plague and violent storm.

His utterances, with their deliberate emphasis and obscure threats, were strategic preliminaries; his systematic destruction and his wholesale throat-cutting were intended primarily as a lesson to his adversaries.
—RENÉ GROUSSET
French historian

Because they virtually grew up on horseback, the Huns were great equestrians. In battle, Hunnic horsemen would often pretend to flee; when pursued, they would suddenly wheel about and release deadly volleys of arrows against their enemies.

Attila as depicted by a 16th-century Italian artist. By the time Attila became coruler of the Huns with his brother Bléda in 434, he was well versed in both war and diplomacy, and the Huns recognized him as their most effective leader.

Like most Christian chroniclers of those days, Socrates Scholasticus always colored his description of events with a strong Christian bias, especially when dealing with non-Christians. He also tended to view the world as a continuous process of miracles. His description of the events of 434 should be viewed in this light. The only piece of information that is truly credible in his story is King Ruga's unexpected death, which naturally seemed a godsend to Theodosius.

King Ruga's sudden death ended the plans for a Hunnic invasion, but it also changed the course of history. It was Ruga's death that enabled Attila to ascend the throne of Hunnia and begin to implement his dream for a world empire.

At the moment of Ruga's death, Attila was already 34 years old, a man of powerful presence who had been preparing himself for the leadership of the Hunnic Empire for well over two decades. Some years later Priscus described Attila as follows: "He was short of stature with a broad chest, massive head, and small eyes. His beard was thin . . . his nose flat, and his complexion swarthy, showing thus the signs of his origin."

In his physical appearance, therefore, Attila was very far from the Roman or German ideal of a leader. At the same time, however, he projected a presence so powerful that very few dared to defy him. Although known for his restraint, fairness, and generosity to his friends, even his closest advisers were sometimes paralyzed with fear in his presence.

In the words of Priscus, the king of the Huns was "haughty in his carriage, casting his eyes about him on all sides so that the proud man's power was to be seen in the very movements of his body." Attila's top commander, Onegesius, could barely bring himself to sit at his table, and Attila's oldest son, Ellák, would seldom dare to look his father in the eye. Moreover, some of the regional rulers of his empire were so intimidated by Attila that they would use whatever means they could to avoid having to attend his court functions. This is demonstrated by the case of King Kurdiak — head of the Akatir tribal federation, which was located between the Don and Volga rivers in the present-day Soviet Union — whom Attila wished to reward for his faithfulness during a rebellion. Kurdiak, however, begged to be excused from this honor. "It would be just as difficult," Priscus reports Kurdiak as saying, "for a mere mortal to be in the presence of a god as it would be to look into the sun."

At the time when he ascended the throne of Hunnia, Attila was already married and had experienced the world as a military commander. His first wife was Arykan, the daughter of a prominent Hunnic tribal chief. Attila had three sons with Arykan: Ellák, Denghizik, and Irnák. Later Attila took many other wives, most of them to seal political alliances, but Arykan always remained his chief wife. Moreover, their three sons remained the only recognized heirs to the throne.

In the late 440s, when he was fighting a new war against the Eastern Roman Empire and preparing a major campaign against the West, Attila dispatched his son Ellák to rule over the Akatir tribal federation as a viceroy. His younger sons, including those from some of his later wives, remained with him. Irnák, his youngest son from Arykan, was his favorite; whereas Attila usually remained unmoved by anyone's presence, he always displayed a special affection for Irnák. Priscus writes that this affection was the result of a prophecy that after Attila's death his empire would fall, then rise again under Irnák.

This legend is a reflection of actual historical events. Following Attila's death, his empire disintegrated in a fratricidal struggle among his sons and the simultaneous rise of the vassal nations. But then Irnák, who is known in Hungarian heroic legends as Prince Csaba, took the remnants of the Huns back to the region between the Black and Caspian seas, where they eventually merged with the ancestors of the Magyars. Together they formed the Hungarian people, who later returned to conquer the heartland of the old Hunnic Empire. The Hungarians of today may only be fragmentary descendants of the Huns, but they still associate themselves with that ancient nation. In the heroic legends of the Hungarians — preserved by the eastern branch of their nation, the Székelys, who live in Transylvania in present-day Romania — they still await the return of Prince Csaba and his Hunnic warriors.

The 420s were years of Attila's preparation for political and military leadership. During that decade he participated in all of his uncle's diplomatic negotiations and military adventures. In the early 420s he was involved in a series of military forays into the Eastern Roman Empire, and in 425 he commanded one of the Hunnic armies, led by King Ruga himself, that tried to install a new emperor of the Western Empire. The 60,000-strong Hunnic army arrived after the pretender to the throne had been killed, but its presence made it possible for Aëtius to install his own man as emperor. Thus Valentinian III became the new ruler of the Western Empire; Aëtius was made governor of Gaul, and his Hunnic friends, including Attila, returned to Hungary with a large tribute in gold.

In 432, Valentinian's mother, Placidia, moved against Aëtius, who fled to the Huns and asked for their help. King Ruga received him like an old friend and promptly sent him back with a large Hunnic army under Attila's command. The result was another Hunnic military victory and an even more favorable political compromise for Aëtius, who was appointed the commander in chief of all Roman armies. He was now the most powerful man in the Western Roman Empire. And Attila was instrumental in his rise.

A portrait of Empress Placidia and her children, Valentinian III and Honoria. Although Valentinian became emperor at the age of six in 425, Placidia ruled the Western Roman Empire in his name until her death in 450; she paid the Huns a large sum in order to secure her son's position on the throne.

At the time of King Ruga's death, Attila was without question the Huns' most gifted military and political leader. Between 434 and 444, however, he still shared royal power with his much weaker older brother Bléda, whose name has been preserved as Buda in Hungarian traditions. If knowledge about Attila's youth is meager, even less is known about Bléda's early life. He is depicted as having been a good-natured but somewhat incompetent leader who usually deferred important decisions to his energetic younger brother. At any rate, Bléda is today best known for having given his name to Hungary's medieval capital, which in 1873 was combined with Pest to form the current capital city of Budapest.

After Ruga's death, Attila and Bléda simply divided the administration of their empire between themselves. This division, however, was done in such a way as to retain both the geographical and the foreign policy unity of the empire. Moreover, unless they were leading major campaigns, the two brothers did not move very far from each other. They remained in constant consultation, making all basic policy decisions jointly.

They began their joint rule by negotiating one of the most important pacts the Huns had ever signed with the Eastern Roman Empire, the Treaty of Margum of 435, the first of many humiliating treaties the Eastern Empire was forced to sign with Attila.

Upon receiving news of the death of King Ruga, who had been planning an invasion of the Eastern Empire, Theodosius II asked to negotiate with the Huns. He immediately sent off two of his best diplomats to meet Attila and Bléda, who received the Eastern Roman envoys under the walls of the city of Margum, situated at the confluence of the Danube and Morava rivers in the northern Balkans. They met the ambassadors on horseback, for "it did not seem proper to the barbarians to confer dismounted," as Priscus put it.

The threat of Hunnic invasion inspired such fear that the Eastern Romans capitulated on almost all counts. The Treaty of Margum obliged Constantinople to repatriate all fugitive tribes and agree not to receive any more refugee tribes or Western Roman defectors, nor enter into alliance with any nation at war with the Huns. Furthermore, Hunnic merchants would enjoy the same rights and privileges as did the Eastern Romans themselves in all of the trading centers along the Hunnic-Roman frontier. Finally, Constantinople agreed to pay 700 pounds of gold per year to the Huns.

As described by Priscus, one of the immediate results of the treaty was that "those who had fled to the [Eastern] Romans were handed back to the barbarians. Among them were the youths Mama and Atakam, scions of the royal house . . . , who [were] crucified [because] of their flight."

The other immediate result of the Treaty of Margum was the coming of peace to the Hunnic-Byzantine frontier, which permitted Attila and Bléda to turn their attention to their northwestern and eastern borders. In a series of campaigns during the late 430s they consolidated their rule over dozens of Germanic, Slavic, and Turkic tribes from the Rhine to the farthest regions of eastern Europe. At the same time they also extended their empire beyond the Caucasus Mountains and the Caspian Sea. The newly conquered peoples included numerous Iranian, Finno-Ugrian, and related Turkic tribes, among them the early Magyars who eventually became the Hungarians of today.

Attila was responsible for most of the eastern campaigns, in the course of which he also reestablished contacts with the so-called White Huns of central Asia, who held sway in the region of the Amu Darya River and the Aral Sea. The White Huns enabled Attila to build good trade relations with such Far Eastern countries as China and India.

Attila's military campaigns in the east went smoothly, largely because many of his opponents simply capitulated. Attila was as famed for his generosity to nations who accepted Hunnic vassalage as he was for his harshness to those who fought against him. As a result, many submitted voluntarily, even happily, to Hunnic overlordship.

It was also helpful that the Huns did not confiscate the lands of their vassal peoples as did the Germans in the conquered provinces of the Western

Roman Empire. Nor did they deprive their new vassals of their own social systems, political traditions, and tribal laws. Moreover, in line with Hunno-Turkic traditions, Attila was also known for his religious tolerance. Unless they rebelled against Hunnic domination, in which case they were severely punished, all conquered peoples enjoyed extensive political, economic, cultural, and religious autonomy. This is clearly evident from the dedicated faithfulness of over a dozen Germanic kings to Attila and the Hunnic imperial idea. Nor were these vassal peoples exploited, for their obligations to the central government consisted only of paying an annual tribute (a kind of federal tax) and of supporting the Huns with auxiliary military forces in case of a major campaign.

Emperor Theodosius and his family watch a chariot race. After a crushing military defeat at the hands of the Huns, Theodosius was forced in 443 to sign the First Peace of Anatolius; among the terms was the payment of 6,000 pounds of gold.

Attila's eastern conquests were concluded by the year 440. The result was a unified and strongly knit Hunnic Empire that stretched from Hungary to central Asia and from the Baltic region to Persia. Attila was now ready to join his brother in harrying the Balkans and western Europe.

When Attila returned to Europe, a new war with Constantinople had already been under way for a year. The immediate cause of the war seems to have been the actions of the bishop of Margum, who apparently crossed the Danube and looted the royal Hunnic tombs. When the Huns demanded the bishop be turned over to them for punishment, Theodosius refused. Meanwhile, the Huns accused the Byzantines of violating the still-fresh Treaty of Margum.

Scholars have suggested that this sword, found in the German village of Althussheim in 1932, is Hunnic in origin. When Attila became sole ruler of the Huns, his discovery of a sword believed to be the legendary Sword of God convinced him that he was invincible in battle.

Attila immediately joined the attack against the Eastern Roman Empire, and one of the first fortresses he encountered was the city of Margum, whose bishop had started the war in the first place. According to the contemporary chronicler Marcellinus Comes, the bishop of Margum, apparently fearing that the inhabitants of the city would turn him over to the Huns, went himself "to the enemy and promised that he would hand over the city . . . if the Scythian [Hunnic] kings made any reasonable proposal." They must have done so, for the bishop promptly "put the city into the hands of its enemies" — and did so without the knowledge of its inhabitants.

The taking of the city of Margum was followed by the conquest of much of the northern Balkans. Attila and Bléda repeated their attacks in the course of the following year, when they "ravaged Illyricum and Thrace." In a series of battles they inflicted crippling defeats on the Eastern Roman armies, and by the autumn of 442 they had taken most of present-day Yugoslavia, Bulgaria, and Greece. Emperor Theodosius was forced to sue for peace.

A treaty was hammered out through the mediation of the Western Romans, who felt they had to come to the aid of their brethren in the east. But Theodosius's military defeat was so complete that not even Ravenna's intervention could secure for him an easy way out. The mediator was Aëtius's son, Carpilio. As described by his grandson, the Roman senator Cassiodorus, Carpilio was less taken by Attila than Aëtius had been: "He found the king [Attila] insolent," wrote Cassiodorus; "so ably did he argue down all his slanderous pretexts for dispute. . . . Thus did he bring back peace which men had despaired."

The new treaty, known as the First Peace of Anatolius, was signed in 443. Under its terms Emperor Theodosius now had to pay the Huns 6,000 pounds of gold for the retreat as well as an annual tribute of 1,000 pounds of gold.

Soon after the Huns' victory over the Eastern Romans, King Bléda died and Attila became the sole ruler of Hunnia. A few decades after Bléda's death several Western sources began to accuse Attila of having killed his brother to unify the Hunnic Empire under his own rule. With the passing of centuries this view became so widespread that after a while even some Hungarian historians began to accept it.

While no one knows the truth, it is worth noting that the best-informed Eastern Roman historians — Priscus, Apollinarus Sidonius, and Theophanes Byzantius — wrote nothing about this alleged fratricide. Neither did the notoriously efficient Byzantine spy system, which made it a point to learn everything about the empire's adversaries.

Whatever the cause of Bléda's death, it coincided with another major event in Hunnic history: the finding of the sacred Sword of God.

They spend their lives on horseback, sometimes astride, sometimes sideways, like women. They hold their meetings thus; they buy and sell, drink and eat—even sleep, lying on the neck of their mounts.
—AMMIANUS MARCELLINUS
Roman soldier and historian

5

The Sword of God

Bléda was laid to rest with the honors due to a king of the Huns. Following his burial, the Huns held a three-day funeral feast, with all the military leaders, vassal kings, and tribal chiefs of the empire in attendance.

After the funeral feast, Attila retired to his bedchamber, where he had an unusual dream. It somehow involved the story of the Sword of God, which his grandfather's shamans used to recite to him, repeating again and again that he should never try to build a world empire without possessing that sword. Now Attila dreamed that an elderly man came down from the sky and handed him the Sacred Sword. Then a sudden whirlwind picked Attila up and carried him over the vast stretches of Europe and Asia. While flying above, he held the Sword of God tightly in his right hand, sometimes slashing it before him. Each time he did so, the trees of the forests would bend, the waters of the rivers and seas would part, and cities and fortifications would topple like piles of sticks.

And so the time passed. The Huns lived peacefully . . . dreaming of an empire that would embrace the world . . . [but knowing that they could never do so] without the help of the Sacred Sword.
—from the legend of the Sacred Sword

Possession of the throne and the Sword of God inspired Attila to march on Constantinople. A series of famines and plagues and a major earthquake had rendered the capital of the Eastern Roman Empire vulnerable to attack.

Attila awoke and summoned the shamans to tell him the meaning of his dream. "The meaning of your dream, my Lord," said Chief Shaman Torda, "is that you shall soon find the Sword of God, and with it you shall conquer the world."

Attila and the Huns knew the story of the Sacred Sword by heart. Yet, they now wished to hear it again from Torda's mouth. And so, the old shaman began the story of the Sacred Sword.

Not even a hundred years had passed, Torda related, before the Huns and the Magyars became so numerous that the land of Meotis was unable to support them. They were forced to find a new homeland once more. So they decided to conquer Scythia.

Soon, even Scythia proved to be too small for them. After some meditation, the leaders of the Huns decided to take their nation westward. The Magyars remained but promised to follow their brethren should they find a suitable homeland.

Before the Huns departed, however, the leaders of the two nations had to decide what to do with the Sword of God, a sacred weapon they had won from the Scythians. After some debate they agreed that it should be handed to a blind man, who should twirl it around seven times and then let it go. Should the sword fall in a westerly direction, the Huns would take it with them. But should it fall toward the east, it would remain with the Magyars.

And so it was done. But then a miracle occurred. Following the seventh spin, the Sacred Sword was caught by a sudden gust of wind that picked it up and swept it toward the west until it was lost from sight.

The Huns began their trek to the west. After many months they finally crossed the Carpathian Mountains and entered beautiful Pannonia. There they clashed with the Germans and the Romans, whom they defeated. And so the time passed. The Huns lived peacefully, dreaming of an empire that would embrace the world but knowing that they could never do so without the help of the Sacred Sword.

Hardly had the old shaman finished his story when suddenly a shepherd boy appeared, bringing an unexpected gift to the king of the Huns. The gift was a magnificent sword of unusual shape and brilliance, which Chief Shaman Torda immediately recognized as the long-lost Sword of God. Attila and the Hunnic leaders were awestruck. The discovery of the Sacred Sword represented a new milestone in the destiny of their nation.

Hungarian heroic legends describe in great detail the story of the Sacred Sword, or Sword of God. But the story of this sword and its impact upon the Huns goes back to ancient times. As described by Attila's contemporary, Priscus,

> When a certain shepherd beheld one heifer of his flock limping . . . , he anxiously followed the trail of blood and at length came to a sword it had unwittingly trampled while nibbling grass. He dug it up and took it straight to Attila. He [Attila] rejoiced at this gift and, being ambitious, thought he had been appointed ruler of the whole world, and that through the sword of Mars supremacy in all wars was assured to him.

The first entry of the Huns into Pannonia. Attila is shown in the left foreground, leading his warriors in the conquest of the former Roman province, which is now part of Hungary, Yugoslavia, and Romania.

Whatever the origins of the Sword of God, its sudden appearance among the Huns in the mid-440s gave a new psychological impetus to Attila's desire to extend his rule over the two Roman empires.

The further deterioration of the Eastern Roman Empire presented him with a golden chance to realize his dream. Conditions in the Byzantine state, already suffering from military defeat and the economic hardship caused by official corruption and the enormous tribute to the Huns, grew still worse in the wake of several natural calamities. These in-

cluded a series of famines and plagues as well as a major earthquake in 447, which destroyed most of the walls and all 47 defensive towers of Constantinople, thereby opening the formerly impregnable imperial city to a possible conquest by the Huns.

Emperor Theodosius recognized the dangers immediately and ordered the fortifications rebuilt as soon as possible. This was done, but the massive project further exhausted the imperial treasury. As a result, the Eastern Romans were unable to pay their annual tribute to the Huns.

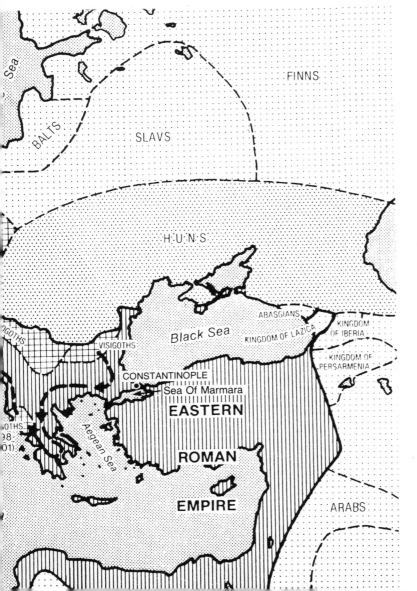

Barbarian tribes had made significant inroads into Europe by the year 400. The arrows show the route taken by the Visigoths, leading to their sack of Rome in 410. Once the Visigoths began to advance, the way was clear for the Huns to close in on Constantinople.

Some of the fortifications built at Constantinople by Emperor Theodosius still stand. The original walls were destroyed by the earthquake of 447 and hastily rebuilt in the face of Attila's advance.

This sparked a new Hunnic-Byzantine war, which quickly turned into a debacle. The Eastern Empire's military outposts in Europe were destroyed, and its Balkan territories were devastated. The Hunnic armies rode unhindered along the Bosporus and the Sea of Marmara, and soon Attila himself stood before the hastily rebuilt walls of Constantinople.

But Attila was denied final victory. Even though the capital lay at the Hun's mercy, he did not take it, apparently because of a new outbreak of plague among its inhabitants. Instead, Attila sent word to Constantinople's besieged emperor that he was willing to sign a new peace treaty.

Emperor Theodosius was in no position to bargain; he had no choice but to accept Attila's terms, which came to be called the Second Peace of Anatolius. The treaty was even more humiliating to the Eastern Romans than the First Peace. In addition to 6,000 pounds of gold that Theodosius had to pay in one lump sum, the annual tribute was now raised to 2,100 pounds of gold. All former Hunnic subjects were to be repatriated and all Roman slaves returned to Hunnia, although the latter could be ransomed for a small sum per person. Even more significant was the treaty's provision that obliged the Eastern

Romans to evacuate all the territories south of the Danube River for a distance of five days' riding. This was Attila's way of preventing the Eastern Romans from rebuilding their fortifications on the Danube, which would have hindered all future Hunnic invasions into the empire.

Having signed the Second Peace of Anatolius, Attila returned home with his victorious armies. Meanwhile, in the reeling Eastern Empire, the hated tax collectors were soon swarming everywhere, amassing money and precious objects for the tribute. Not even churches, monasteries, or members of the clergy were spared. Nevertheless, a great deal of the treasure collected never found its way to the Huns; much of it was pocketed instead by corrupt Byzantine officials.

Soon after Attila's return home, the tribute and the annual tax began to flow into Hunnia. But this flow soon slowed to a trickle, which greatly angered Attila, who sent several envoys to Constantinople to urge faster compliance with its treaty obligations. Theodosius replied by arguing for a reduction in the obligations.

Hunnic warriors overran the Roman defenses in Europe, but a plague prevented them from taking Constantinople. Even though the city was spared, Emperor Theodosius was obliged to sign another humiliating peace treaty with Attila.

In order to pay tribute to the Huns, the Romans were forced to assess heavy taxes. Corrupt officials often pocketed the revenues, angering both the taxpayers and the Huns.

Finally, in the early part of 449, Attila dispatched a high-level embassy to Constantinople. It was led jointly by Edeco, the commander of Attila's guard regiments, and the accomplished diplomat Orestes, a Pannonian Roman whose son would later become the last Western Roman emperor.

These two men were known to dislike and distrust each other. Orestes viewed Edeco as an upstart barbarian, while Edeco regarded Orestes as a scheming adventurer. Such relationships were fairly common in the Hunnic royal court, where Attila relied on the services of many nationalities. But he turned such relationships to his advantage by using the mutual distrust of his chief advisers to make sure that none of them would betray him. Thus it was no accident that he placed this important embassy under the joint leadership of Edeco and Orestes.

The Hunnic ambassadors were received in the imperial palace amid the appropriate pomp and fanfare. Edeco personally handed Attila's letter to Theodosius and orally repeated Attila's demands for compliance with the terms of the treaty. Following their reception, Attila's two ambassadors were separated. While Orestes was taken to his quarters, Edeco was given a guided tour of the imperial palace by Bigilas, a renegade Goth interpreter.

The residence of the Eastern Roman emperors at Constantinople was in those days the most impressive and luxurious palace in the world. It certainly made a great impression upon Edeco, who did not even attempt to conceal his amazement at what he saw. Bigilas immediately reported his observations to his superior, Lord Chamberlain Chrysaphius, who since 443 had been virtually in charge of the whole imperial court.

Based on Bigilas's observation, Chrysaphius came to the conclusion that Edeco had been seduced by the luxury of the imperial palace and would be willing to enter the Byzantines' employ. Chrysaphius invited the Hun to a private dinner, where he learned that Edeco had personal access to Attila. Soon the lord chamberlain was offering Edeco riches, titles, and imperial service if he would arrange for the assassination of the king of the Huns. Edeco played along, asking for an advance of 50 pounds of gold to be used for bribing his subordinates. He also asked that the gold be sent after him, perhaps by Bigilas, so as to divert all possible suspicions. This was Edeco's way of protecting himself while at the same time supplying Attila with ready evidence of the plot. Thus, Chrysaphius fell into the trap of the still shrewder Edeco.

It was decided that the emperor, who approved Chrysaphius's assassination plot, would send a new embassy to Attila, to be headed by the universally respected Maximinius, who would not be told of the plot. The other members of Maximinius's embassy to the court of the Huns included Bigilas and Priscus, the historian and philosopher who later wrote an eight-volume history of his era in which he also included a long account of his experiences in Hunnia.

The Hunnic and the Byzantine envoys left Constantinople at the same time. They traveled together and at times even ate together. One such joint session, however, led to an argument in which Bigilas declared that "it was not fitting to compare a god [Theodosius] and a man [Attila]." The Huns became quite upset and were pacified only when "Maximinius flattered Edeco and Orestes with gifts of silken garments and Indian gems." Finally, the two parties crossed into Hunnic territory just east of present-day Belgrade, Yugoslavia. The two groups separated, the Huns continuing 25 miles north to Attila's camp while the Byzantines remained behind.

When Edeco arrived at the Huns' camp he told Attila about the Byzantine assassination plot. Several days later, the Eastern Romans were summoned. Attila received them in his tent, sitting on a wooden throne. Concealing his knowledge of the plot but unable to conceal his anger, the king of the Huns lashed out at Bigilas, calling him a "shameless beast" and ordering him to return to Constantinople.

Bigilas immediately set off for the Byzantine capital, but he was so completely fooled that he decided to take his 16-year-old son along when he returned to Attila's camp. Lord Chamberlain Chrysaphius, for his part, was so jubilant at the prospects that he doubled the promised bribe to 100 pounds of gold.

Upon his return to the Hunnic capital, Bigilas and his followers were immediately arrested and confronted with the evidence. Threatened with the death of his young son, Bigilas confessed everything. Attila, realizing that the Goth interpreter was only a small player in this imperial plot, permitted Bigilas's son to return to Constantinople and ransomed his father for 50 pounds of gold.

Attila's goal was to humble Emperor Theodosius. He sent a new embassy to Constantinople that included both Orestes and Edeco. They were instructed to return the assassination payment directly to the emperor and to tell him the following in the presence of the whole imperial court:

> Theodosius is the son of a nobly born father; and so is Attila. But while Attila has preserved the nobility he had inherited from his father, Mundzuk, Theodosius had lost his own, for he became Attila's tributary and therefore his slave. But even as a slave Theodosius acted dishonorably, for he had secretly conspired against the life of his master. And Attila will not cease blaming those who have conspired against him until Theodosius will hand over [Chrysaphius] for punishment.

No Roman emperor had ever been so shamed as was Theodosius after his botched plot on Attila's life. The emperor, at Chrysaphius's urging, chose

An engraving shows Attila receiving a delegation from Theodosius. When Attila discovered that Theodosius had bribed one of the interpreters to assassinate him, he used this information to further humiliate the emperor.

to accept responsibility and try to appease the king of the Huns. He sent to Attila a group of the highest-ranking ambassadors bearing lavish presents and word that the Eastern Roman Empire would fully abide by the Second Peace.

Attila showed leniency, agreeing to be satisfied simply with the full implementation of the terms of the Second Peace of Anatolius; for the time being he gave up the idea of Chrysaphius's extradition. Furthermore, he indicated that in the future he might even evacuate the Byzantine territories to the south of the Danube.

Attila's commander, Onegesius, and the king's oldest son, Ellák, the viceroy of the eastern part of Attila's empire, appeared at the Hunnic capital at about this time. They had just returned from the east, where their armies had crushed all opposition. Thus, for the first time, Attila was assured complete internal control over all his territory. Now, with the Byzantines defeated and the Sword of God at his side, he was ready to take the next step in the building of a gigantic empire: the conquest of the northern Mediterranean world.

6

Showdown at Catalaunum

The year 450 proved to be momentous in the fortunes of the two Roman states and Attila's Hunnic Empire. In July of that year Emperor Theodosius of Constantinople fell from his horse and died without an heir. For a while his elderly unmarried sister, Pulcheria, tried to take the helm of the empire; then, in order to save the dynasty, she married an aging Illyrian general by the name of Marcian, who in 450 became the new Eastern Roman emperor. One of Emperor Marcian's first decisions was to cancel the terms of the Second Peace of Anatolius and refuse to pay the annual tribute to Attila.

Attila, meanwhile, was mulling over a marriage offer made in January 450 by Honoria, the 32-year-old sister of the Western Roman emperor Valentinian III. She even sent a ring to the king of the Huns, proclaiming herself betrothed to him and asking him to come and free her from her brother's clutches. Honoria's unexpected marriage proposal had far-reaching implications.

In war itself, he is prominent less as a captain than as a leader of men.
—RENÉ GROUSSET
French historian

A 19th-century painting of Attila marching toward Paris. The Huns' invasion of Gaul took the Romans by surprise, and Attila's forces captured several major cities before being stopped 80 miles from Paris.

Honoria, the sister of Emperor Valentinian, wrote to Attila and offered to be his wife. When Valentinian then forced his sister to marry another man, Attila demanded that Honoria be released from her marriage and that he himself be given a voice in ruling the Roman Empire.

Honoria, born in 418, had grown up in Constantinople amid the mystical-religious surroundings of the Byzantine court (she had arrived there at the age of six after her family fled the warfare caused by the struggle for the Western Roman throne in 425). Her family persuaded Honoria to take the vow of chastity when she was still a young girl, in the hope that her devotion to God would gain divine help in restoring her family to the throne. Her family may also have pushed her into a life of celibacy to prevent her from contracting an early marriage and producing a child who might become a rival for the Western Roman throne.

After the rise of her brother, Valentinian, to the emperorship, Honoria was given the imperial title of Augusta. She continued to be reared for a religious life, but as she grew to womanhood it became evident that she was not cut out to be a nun; she had inherited her mother's sensual nature. Honoria was still in her teens when she began a romantic relationship with Eugenius, the steward of the imperial household. When the affair was discovered,

Eugenius was executed. Honoria was exiled to Constantinople for a life of repentance.

We do not know how long Honoria's exile lasted, but in a few years she was back at the Western court in Ravenna. Outwardly, she appeared to have accepted her fate, but in fact she was only waiting for an opportune moment to free herself. This came in the year 450, when through the services of an imperial servant, Hyacinthus, she was able to dispatch a letter to Attila asking him to take her as his wife.

When Valentinian learned of his sister's action, he became furious. He ordered the messenger Hyacinthus tortured and executed. Then he deprived Honoria of her rank and forced her to marry an insignificant imperial administrator by the name of Flavius Bassus Herculanus.

Honoria's offer must have puzzled Attila, but he soon realized that championing her cause could help him implement his plans for the expansion of his empire. In the fall of 450 he dispatched a letter to Emperor Valentinian, demanding that Honoria be freed from her forced marriage to Flavius Bassus,

Emperor Valentinian III (425–55) was on his own after the death of his mother, Placidia, in 450. Whereas Placidia had always taken pains to keep peace with the Huns, Valentinian quickly adopted a more provocative attitude toward Attila. Subsequent events bore out the wisdom of Placidia's policy.

restored to her rank, and sent to him as his bride. Moreover, Attila suggested that as Honoria's future husband he should be given a role in running the affairs of the Western Roman Empire.

Valentinian refused to comply with Attila's demands — which was exactly what the king of the Huns had expected; now the Huns had a pretext for a future invasion of the Western Empire. In his response to Attila, Valentinian pointed out that his sister was already married and therefore could hardly be Attila's betrothed. Moreover, being a woman, under Roman law she had no legal right to share in political power. This, of course, was not entirely true, for many women had wielded power in the empire, and Valentinian himself had succeeded to the throne through the female line.

Valentinian's rejection of Attila's demands happened to coincide with an outbreak of fighting within the Ripuarian Frankish Confederation on the Rhine, part of Attila's Hunnic Empire. After the Frankish king's death, both of his sons claimed his throne, the older one appealing to Attila for help, the younger one turning to Aëtius and the Western Romans. Attila seized on the older son's appeal as another pretext for invading the Western Empire.

Attila put his plan of conquest in motion in late 450, moving on Gaul with the help of Genseric, king of the Vandals. In their way stood the armies of Aëtius and King Theodoric of the Visigoths. The two sides were fated to meet in combat south of Catalaunum (now Châlons-sur-Marne), in the most famous yet least successful of Attila's many battles.

Attila's army marched westward out of Hunnia, gathering strength as it went. Subject nationalities joined the march, adding large amounts of well-preserved food and live animals for nourishment, vast stores of arms, river-crossing equipment, and siege machines, swelling the force to an enormous size. Onegesius and Ellák supervised the training of the massive multinational armed units, whose members spoke many different languages, to act in concert on the battlefield. But Attila was soon to find out that it was one thing to lead a well-disciplined Hunnic army composed of highly trained cavalry

Above all, curiously enough, characteristic of this leader of hordes was his frequent use of cunning and political tactics in preference to war . . . which led him to seek diplomatic pretexts for his actions, in accordance with formal practice, so that he might at any rate appear to have right on his side.
—RENÉ GROUSSET
French historian

units, yet quite another to lead a huge multinational and multilingual army that also included infantry units unfamiliar with Hunnic fighting strategies and tactics.

By early 451, Aëtius knew that Attila was moving westward, but the Roman had no idea where the actual invasion would occur. Would it be Gaul or Italy? Because of this uncertainty, Aëtius refused to leave Italy until Attila was already well into Gaul. At the same time, he managed to seal a temporary alliance with his lifelong rival and enemy, King Theodoric of the Visigoths, to join forces with him against their common foe.

Roman cavalry troops attack mounted Sarmatians. When Attila recruited the Huns' subject peoples, such as the Sarmatians, to form one of the largest armies the world had seen, he may not have realized that an army made up of diverse nationalities could be hard to manage in the heat of battle.

Most contemporary sources and even many modern works describe Attila's Grand Army as a force of at least a half million men. Given contemporary travel and supply conditions, however, this is undoubtedly an overstatement. His army was probably 250,000 strong, which still made it one of the largest forces that the world had seen until those days. It consisted of about 100,000 cavalrymen (mostly Hunnic), about an equal number of Germanic infantry (Gepids, Ostrogoths, Ripuarian Franks, Herulians, Squirians, as well as various Longobard, Saxon, Marcomanni, Alemanni, and Rugian bands), and perhaps half as many other auxiliaries, including Alans, Slavs, and various Sarmatian groups.

Before crossing the Rhine, Attila divided his forces into three separate army groups. The main group under his command crossed the Rhine in late February or early March 451 and then followed the beautiful Moselle Valley through present-day Luxembourg right into France. The memory of Attila's passing is still preserved in the name of the majestic mountain ridge that follows the river on its southeastern flank: Hunsrück, or the Huns' Ridge.

Attila's invasion of Gaul produced mass panic among the country's inhabitants. He conquered city after city — Metis (present-day Metz), Virdunumon (Verdun), Durocortorum (Reims), Tricassis (Troyes) — in his relentless march west. His conquests in the spring and summer of 451 gave birth to a number of legends blaming him for all sorts of barbaric acts, even though we now know that most of them had nothing to do with him or his army. It was during the post-Attilan centuries that these much-embellished stories were attached to him, after they had already been reshaped by the early medieval imagination into tales of miraculous salvation.

An example of such a tale is the legend of St. Nicasius, the bishop of Reims, who was allegedly martyred by Attila. When everyone fled the city, so the story goes, Nicasius and his sister Eutropia refused to do so. They waited for Attila in full regalia in front of the Reims cathedral, singing one of King David's psalms, only to be cut down cruelly and mer-

Although Aëtius grew up among the Huns and was a childhood friend of Attila's, he agreed to lead the Roman forces defending Gaul. Despite his loyal service, he was eventually put to death by Valentinian, who always considered him a dangerous rival.

cilessly by the king of the Huns himself. Nicasius's head, separated from his body, toppled onto the cobblestones — yet its mouth continued to sing the psalm. The horrified Huns fled the city in panic — a remarkable story, but according to contemporary sources St. Nicasius and his sister perished at the hands of the Vandals nearly a half century *before* Attila's invasion of Gaul.

By May 451 Attila reached the important city of Aurelianum (Orléans) on the Loire River, about 80 miles south of Paris, and laid siege, expecting the city to fall like all the other cities before it. Then, suddenly and unexpectedly, the Roman-Visigothic army appeared.

For once, Attila was caught by surprise; up to then he had been convinced that the age-old animosity between the Romans and the Visigoths and the personal rivalry between Aëtius and King Theodoric would keep those two from joining forces. The Hunnic army was not prepared to fight a pitched battle against so large an opposing force, so Attila ordered a 100-mile retreat to the east. There, on the Catalaunian Plains, he regrouped his army and waited to face the Roman and Visigothic forces. The time to do battle had come.

This engraving shows St. Lupus, bishop of Troyes, pleading with Attila to spare the city. Attila acceded to the bishop's plea, but local legends still portray him as a cruel and merciless barbarian.

It was late June or early July, a quarter million of Attila's men facing an equal number of Romans and Visigoths, lined up opposite each other for four miles in the summer heat. The battle did not last long, going from midafternoon until late into the night, and in the end it resulted in one of the highest single-day losses of human life the world had ever seen or would see for many centuries thereafter. The chronicler Jordanes noted that "165,000 are said to have been slain on both sides"; that is, a total of 330,000 men. Idatius, on the other hand, used the more modest figure of 300,000. Both of these figures represent the customary exaggerations of medieval chroniclers. But even more somber modern scholars recognize the unusual scope of the slaughter and speak of tens of thousands of dead, perhaps in the vicinity of 100,000.

This huge loss of human life was partially the result of the size of the combatants' armies but also partially of Attila's inability to follow the customary Hunnic strategy. Because of his rapid withdrawal from Orléans and the equally rapid appearance of the Roman-led forces, he had no time to deploy his Hunnic cavalry on the flanks of his armed forces. As a result, his crack Hunnic horsemen were penned into the middle of the four-mile-long battlefront and were thus left immobile to die in hand-to-hand combat before the onrushing Roman-Visigothic forces.

The bodies piled up in mounds as the warriors continued to hack and hew, knee deep in the gore of the fallen of both armies. The battle came to a halt only when total darkness descended on the Catalaunian Plains and when total exhaustion forced both sides to retire to their own side of the battle-field. It was only at dawn the next day that the leaders of the rival armies realized the full extent of their losses. The battlefield was strewn with tens of thousands of dead, the air filled with the screams of the dying and the wounded, who needed to be collected and cared for. Neither side could muster the strength to start a new attack; they simply stood and faced each other, separated by mountains of corpses and moaning human wrecks.

Not even Attila had witnessed a massacre of such proportions before. Nor had Aëtius and his allies, who finally decided to abandon the battlefield. The desire to leave was especially strong among the Visigoths, who appear to have suffered the most grievous losses — including that of their leader, King Theodoric, whose butchered body was found only after an intensive search led by his two sons.

Attila waited only long enough for Aëtius's army to leave the field, then ordered his own armies to retreat. Thus ended the Battle of the Catalaunian Plains. Attila had suffered a great setback, his plans for the conquest of Gaul dashed, at least for the moment. For the first time in his life he had been unable to gain a clear victory.

> *The result of the battle of the Catalaunian Plains was to force Attila out of Gaul, but entirely because of Aëtius' maneuverings, the battle did not end the Hunnish menace as easily as it might have.*
> —ISAAC ASIMOV
> from *The Dark Ages*

7

The Scourge of God

Attila's ill-fated invasion of Gaul was meant to be the first step in his conquest — guaranteed by his possession of the Sword of God and by the dictate of heaven — of the two Roman empires. But his campaign in Gaul did not end the way he hoped it would. Forced to return home without victory, Attila found his veneer of invincibility shattered, and perhaps even he himself began to have doubts about his mission as the designated unifier of humankind.

Attila had to do something fast in order to remove any doubt that he was not the select of God. One year after his unsuccessful invasion of Gaul, he turned against Italy, the very heart of the Western Roman Empire. If he were successful, he planned to follow up with an attack against the Eastern Romans.

Attila's progress into Italy has been the subject of much scholarly curiosity, widespread speculation, and any number of bad historical films.
—EDWARD PETERS
American historian

A 16th-century Italian medal commemorating the destruction of Aquileia in northern Italy portrays Attila with horns and pointed ears. After being checked in Gaul, Attila decided to renew his attack on the Western Roman Empire by invading Italy itself.

Although Attila's adversaries immediately began to portray the Battle of the Catalaunian Plains as a defeat for the Hunnic king — a claim also made by most modern historians — the events of the year 452 clearly show that Attila's armies were hardly a defeated military force. As the Huns prepared a campaign of massive proportions, the Western Romans stood by and did nothing; apparently, they had been so exhausted by their efforts in Gaul that they were unable to take even a nominal stand against Attila. The Visigoths, too, had ceased to be a significant power after their encounter with Attila in 451. The Hunnic armies had so weakened their ranks that they were forced to relinquish preeminence in Gaul to their northern rivals, the Salian Franks. Thus, the Franks emerged as the most important Germanic people of Gaul; they even gave their name to that province, which came to be called France.

Attila's new invading army of the year A.D. 452 was large — probably around 100,000 men — but not nearly as large as his Grand Army of the previous year. The reason for this was not the lack of manpower, for the ranks of the Huns were being constantly replenished by new waves of invaders from central Asia. Rather, it was Attila's realization that he could achieve much more with a smaller, well-organized, and well-disciplined army than with a larger one that was impossible to control.

Emperor Valentinian and Aëtius lacked the military strength to make a stand against Attila, nor could they look for any meaningful help from Emperor Marcian of the Eastern Empire or King Thorismond of the Visigoths. The only hope Valentinian and Aëtius had was that the siege of the northern Italian cities would slow Attila down enough to prevent him from carrying the war to Ravenna and to Rome — the latter still being the center of Western Christendom. But Aëtius recognized that as a slim possibility at best; he proposed that the center of the Western Roman government be shifted from Italy to Gaul, which Attila would be unlikely to reinvade in the foreseeable future.

However, Emperor Valentinian refused. He distrusted Aëtius almost as much as he distrusted Attila himself, particularly in light of Aëtius's earlier friendship with the Huns. And his refusal to give his daughter in marriage to Aëtius's son worsened the two leaders' relationship still more. Ultimately, their mutual animosity would lead Valentinian to order Aëtius's assassination in 454.

Valentinian departed Ravenna for Rome and hoped for the best. Shortly thereafter, in the spring of 452, Attila's armies began their march. They crossed the passes of the Julian Alps in May of that year and descended upon the Lombard Plain near Aquileia. Located between present-day Venice and Trieste on the northernmost point of the Adriatic Sea, Aquileia was a heavily fortified city, which for many centuries had served as the defensive bastion of northeastern Italy. In addition to its heavy fortifications, it was also surrounded by the waters of the Natisone River, and as such it was very difficult

A 16th-century woodcut shows the storks fleeing Aquileia. Ancient historians reported that when Attila's troops grew discouraged with the long siege, he rallied them by claiming that the storks knew that the city was about to fall.

to take. Attila, however, was determined to capture this key fortress before proceeding deeper into Italy.

The Huns laid siege to Aquileia, but after nearly three months the city seemed as impregnable as ever. Attila was about to break camp and move on into Italy's interior when, according to Priscus, he saw something that made him change his mind:

> Attila chanced to be walking around the walls . . . and noticed that . . . the storks, who build their nests in the gables of houses, were bearing their young from the city and, contrary to their custom, were carrying them into the country. Being a very shrewd observer of events, he understood this and said to his sol-

diers: "You see the birds foresee the future. They are leaving the city sure to perish. . . . Do not think this a meaningless or uncertain sign; fear, arising from the things they foresee, has changed their custom." Why say more? He inflamed the hearts of the soldiers to attack Aquileia again.

His soldiers believed what Attila told them, that the storks were fleeing the city. And so on August 23, 452, Aquileia was stormed, taken, plundered, and totally destroyed. Thus Attila sent a message to the citizens of the other northern Italian cities in his path: Open your gates voluntarily and accept my rule, or suffer the same fate as Aquileia.

Tradition has it that those Aquileians who survived the carnage fled to a series of small islands in the Adriatic. There they founded several new settlements, which gradually merged to form the great city of Venice. Venice, however, is not alone in tracing its roots back to Attila's invasion of Italy; many other northern Italian cities and towns connect their origins to the conquests of the king of the Huns.

The news of Aquileia's fall and destruction spread terror throughout northern Italy. Many cities simply opened their gates at the approach of Attila and accepted Hunnic suzerainty. The largest and richest of the cities of the Lombard Plain, Mediolanum — known today as Milan — was among those that cooperated with the Huns and gladly accepted taxation in lieu of destruction. Other cities, meanwhile, still refused to open their gates. Invariably, they were captured and destroyed, and all their inhabitants were put to the sword.

The surrender of Milan produced a memorable story. Allegedly, upon entering the imperial palace of that city, Attila's gaze fell on a large mural that depicted the rulers of the Western and Eastern Roman empires on their golden thrones, gazing down upon the bodies of slain Huns lying in front of them. Attila was so enraged by this portrayal that he immediately ordered a local court artist to repaint the mural. In this new version, it was Attila sitting on the golden throne, and in front of him were the two Roman emperors holding sacks of gold and pouring their contents at the feet of the king of the Huns.

In light of Attila's successful conquest of northern Italy, Valentinian and Aëtius fell into despair. With no other option open to them, they decided to send an embassy to Attila and beg for peace. And knowing how sensitive the king of the Huns was about the composition of an embassy, they selected the most prominent men available to them. It was headed by Pope Leo I himself, who came in full regalia and with the moral power of the Christian world behind him. St. Prosper of Aquitaine, who served as Pope Leo's secretary and wrote a chronicle of his times, described the result:

Pope Leo I (right center) led a delegation from Rome to sue for peace with Attila. The king of the Huns agreed to withdraw from Italy in return for a large sum of money, while reserving the right to launch another invasion in the future. The invasion never came because Attila died a year later.

In all the deliberations of the emperor, the senate, and the Roman people nothing better was found than to send an embassy to the terrible king and ask for peace. Relying on the help of God, . . . the most blessed Pope Leo undertook these negotiations. . . . Nor did it turn out otherwise than faith had expected. The king received the whole delegation courteously, and he was so flattered by the presence of the highest priest that he ordered his men to stop the hostilities and, promising peace, returned beyond the Danube.

St. Prosper neglected to say that there was a dear price for Attila's withdrawal. Valentinian had to pay a huge sum to Attila, resume the payment of an annual tribute to him, and grant him the largely honorific title of *magister militium*, or commander in chief. Furthermore, Attila demanded that Honoria be sent to him, or else he would return once more to claim her. Whatever Attila's goal may have been with this promise, he certainly left the door open for a new invasion of Italy.

Most historians believe that Attila's decision not to pursue his campaign to central Italy and Rome itself was due less to Pope Leo's influence than to such factors as the lack of food for his armies, scarcity of fodder for his horses, and a recurrent epidemic that usually haunted large armies during long summer campaigns. But a more colorful explanation is given in a Hungarian folktale to explain why Attila did not lay siege to Rome.

According to the tale, Attila was weighing the pros and cons of an attack on Rome when, one night, he had a dream. In the dream he met the Apostles St. Peter and St. Paul, who told him that God did not wish him to conquer the Eternal City. The Apostles also informed Attila that God had grown tired of all the bloodletting and was withdrawing Attila's commission to be his scourge.

Attila's vision of Saints Peter and Paul, as painted by the Renaissance master Raphael. According to legend, Attila had a dream in which the two Apostles told him that God did not want him to conquer Rome.

The next day, as was his custom, Attila called his shamans together and asked them about the meaning of his dream. They all agreed that it was indeed God who had sent him this message and for this reason he should give up the idea of conquering Rome. Otherwise, they told him, he might well share the fate of the Visigothic king Alaric, who died under mysterious circumstances soon after conquering and sacking Rome in 410.

Attila's successful invasion of Italy, coming as it did after his less-than-successful invasion of Gaul, was certainly an indication that he had recovered from the Battle of the Catalaunian Plains. At the same time, Attila also seems to have decided that he would have to go about the conquest of the known world piecemeal, leading alternating campaigns against Rome and Constantinople. Now, withdrawing from northern Italy to the Hunnic capital in present-day Hungary, he planned another invasion, against the Eastern Roman Empire.

That next invasion, however, never took place. Just before the start of the next campaign season in the spring of 453, Attila decided to take another wife. It is almost certain that this marriage, to Ildikó, was simply another of his political marriages, for a man of his stature did not have to marry a woman to gain her for himself. Priscus reported that Ildikó was both young and beautiful, and it is therefore possible that she captured the fancy of the king, who was already in his mid-fifties. Attila may even have fallen in love with her. Emotions, however, must have played only a secondary consideration in the mind of a man whose horizon was limited only by the farthest extent of the three neighboring continents.

Attila's wedding ended in tragedy, its celebration in a funeral feast. With his death the two Roman empires were saved, and his dream of an all-encompassing Hun-dominated world vanished into nothingness. Attila's death was followed by a period of silence and then by a vicious civil war that soon tore apart his entire empire.

8

The Huns After Attila

Attila had many wives, so it is quite likely he also had many sons. Of these, however, we know of only six. Among them were his three sons given birth to by Arykan, his first wife: Ellák, Denghizik, and Irnák, the only sons with the right of succession. But there were also Emnetzúr and Ultzindúr, two sons from another Hunnic wife, and Giesmus, his only son by the daughter of King Ardaric of the Gepidae.

Although Attila had clearly indicated that he wanted his oldest son, Ellák, to succeed him as the sole ruler of his empire, his other sons disagreed. They began to bicker over succession almost immediately after having buried their father. This soon led to armed clashes, which in turn permitted several of the subject nations to rise against the Huns. Led by the capable King Ardaric, who at one time was one of Attila's closest advisers, the anti-Hunnic coalition soon inflicted several major defeats on the fragmented and disoriented Huns, and in so doing ended the unity of Attila's once-mighty empire. According to Jordanes:

Thus did the Huns give way, a race to which men thought the whole world must yield.
—JORDANES
on the Huns' defeat at
the Nedao

The Holy Crown of Hungary, which dates from the 11th century. Although modern scholars question the existence of a direct link between the nation of Hungary and the ancient Huns, Attila lives on in Hungarian tradition as a visionary leader and a benefactor of his people.

The sons of Attila, who through the license of his lust formed almost a people of themselves, were clamoring that the nations should be divided among them equally and that warlike kings with their people should be apportioned to them by lot like a family estate. When Ardaric, king of the Gepidae, learned this, he became enraged because so many nations were being treated like slaves, and was the first to rise against the sons of Attila. . . . They took up arms against the destruction that menaced all and joined battle with the Huns of Pannonia, near the river called Nedao. . . .

Finally, after many bitter conflicts, victory fell unexpectedly to the Gepidae. By the sword and conspiracy Ardaric destroyed almost 30,000. . . . In this battle fell Ellac, the elder son of Attila. . . . His remaining brothers were put to flight near the shore of the Sea of Pontus. . . . Thus did the Huns give way, a race to which men thought the whole world must yield.

Notwithstanding the death of Ellák and the rapid fragmentation of Attila's empire, the Huns continued to wield some power for about 15 years. Attila's second son, Denghizik, still controlled parts of present-day Hungary and much of the Pontic steppes north of the Black Sea, right up to the Don River. He also led several campaigns against the rebellious German tribes as well as against the Eastern Roman Empire. But being impetuous and lacking his father's ability and charisma, most of Denghizik's campaigns failed.

Denghizik was also hindered by the absence of his father's able generals. Onegesius probably died during Attila's invasion of Gaul, while the equally capable Orestes, seeing the collapse of Attila's empire, offered his services to the Western Roman emperor, who appointed him commander in chief of the Western Roman armies. Later, Orestes was able to place his own son, Romulus Augustulus (475–476), on the Western Roman throne. Thus did the son of one of Attila's generals become the last ruler of the empire Attila had hoped to destroy.

The end of the Hunnic Empire came in 469 when, after his unsuccessful invasion of Thrace, Denghizik was defeated and killed. As recorded in the contemporary Chronicle of the Lamb: "Dinzirichus, Attila's son, was killed . . . in Thrace. His head was brought to Constantinople, carried in procession through the Middle Street, and fixed on a pole at the Wooden Circus. The whole city turned out to look at it."

Irnák, Attila's youngest son, who is known in Hungarian legends as Prince Csaba, survived both of his brothers as well as the demise of his father's empire. He made peace with Byzantine emperor Leo I (457–74) and then settled with a small group of his people in the area of present-day Bulgaria. It was an irony of fate that Leo granted Irnák the very same territory that Attila had destroyed and depopulated some three decades earlier. There the Huns were later absorbed by the people of the Balkans, including the related Bulgarians, who settled in that region some 200 years after the collapse of Attila's empire.

A plate from the helmet of Agilulf, king of the Lombards (590–616). After Attila's empire broke up, the Lombards were among the many peoples who continued to attack the Roman Empire. The Western Roman Empire finally fell to the Goths in 476.

The brothers Géza and Ladislas were 11th-century warrior-kings who promoted Christianity in Hungary. By portraying them in the midst of a stag hunt, the authors of the Viennese Illuminated Chronicle clearly meant to link them with Hunor and Magor, the legendary founders of the Huns.

Irnák faded out of history, but as Prince Csaba he remained very much part of the Hungarian legends, where he occupies a very special place even today. According to Magister Simon Kézai's 13th-century work *Deeds of the Hungarians*, Csaba fought two battles with his brother Aladár (actually King Ardaric of the Gepids). Csaba won the first battle but lost the second, which "lasted for 15 days" and in which "so much German blood was spilled" that "it was impossible to drink from the Danube." According to Kézai, 3,000 of the Huns who escaped the Second Battle of Krimhild settled down on the Field of Csigle in Transylvania, but fearing the Germans "they called themselves Sakuli [Székely], not Huns."

Later this legend evolved into a much more complex story, wherein Prince Csaba became endowed with supernatural powers. According to this version of the legend, it was actually Prince Csaba who had settled the Sakuli/Székely in Transylvania. Upon his departure he told the Huns there that should they ever be attacked by an enemy, he would always return to save them. He and his warriors would appear in the sky, galloping along the Milky Way.

For centuries the Hungarian-speaking Székelys of Transylvania, which became part of Romania in 1920, believed in this legend. After each calamity that threatened them — such as the plan of Romania's Communist dictator, Nicolae Ceauşescu, during the 1970s and 1980s, to bulldoze their villages and suppress their language — they always attributed their survival to Prince Csaba's miraculous intervention.

Attila, too, has lived on in the imagination, and today, 1,500 years after his death, his name is known throughout the world. How he is remembered, however, varies from culture to culture. In the English-speaking world, which has derived its information mostly from French, Italian, and Scandinavian sources, he is known as an unspeakably cruel and destructive barbarian. In much of the German-speaking world, however, his name is associated with medieval courtly life and with a military might that was the envy of the contemporary world. At the same time, in Hungary, the country with the closest ties to Hunnic traditions, Attila is a national hero whose personality embodies everything that is noble, heroic, and majestic in the history of a nation.

Whichever approach one takes in looking at Attila's role in history, one must acknowledge that his true personality has been altered significantly both by anti-Hunnic propaganda and by romantic idealization. It took more than a century of historical scholarship to unravel some of the mysteries surrounding this great conqueror and to come up with a kind of consensus about his personality and his role in history.

The pioneer in this effort was the French historian Amedée Thierry, who during the 1850s and 1860s divided the traditions surrounding Attila into two categories: first, the Christian-Roman tra-

> *The personality of Attila had been the sole bond of the Huns, and the ensuing struggle for leadership among his successors and an uprising of several subject Germanic peoples in 454 led to the final destruction of the Huns at the battle of Nedao.*
> —EDWARD PETERS
> American historian

ditions, which portray the Hunnic king as a cruel, bloody, and inhuman tyrant who was God's curse upon the world; and second, the pagan-Germanic traditions, which describe him as a humane, understanding, wise, and occasionally even somewhat complacent ruler. Although Thierry dealt relatively little with Hungarian traditions, and although later historians have adjusted his categorization somewhat, his basic approach is still valid today.

Thierry's so-called Christian-Roman traditions about Attila are found mostly in French and Italian religious legends. All of these pious stories display the Western church's intense dislike of the pagan Hunnic king. All of them try to demonstrate the unarmed church's ultimate victory over the armed barbarian, and all of them tend to attribute this victory to various miraculous and divine interventions. These religiously inspired stories include, among others, the Legend of St. Lupus of Troyes, wherein the saintly bishop persuades the conqueror to spare his city; the Legend of St. Auctor of Metz, where the Cathedral of St. Stephen is saved by God through inflicting temporary blindness upon the Huns; the Legend of St. Nicasius of Reims, where the Huns are forced to flee upon seeing the saint's decapitated head continuing to sing King David's psalms; the Legend of St. Ursula, whose martyrdom, along with that of "11,000 other virgins," saves the city of Cologne from destruction; the Legend of St. Johannes of Ravenna, where the appearance of the saintly archbishop "in company of Jesus Christ" forces the Huns to abandon the city; and the Legend of St. Geminianus of Modena, whose city is also saved by the Huns' temporary blindness, inflicted upon them by God.

While each of these legends may contain a grain of truth, they are all strongly propagandistic in nature, and as such reflect very little about the true personality of Attila. They simply display the official attitude of the militant church against pagan barbarism, and are based on the popular presumption that Attila was an evil barbarian who simply served as God's instrument to punish the sinful Christian world. Christian authors routinely distorted reality

A 15th-century painting of St. Ursula. According to Christian tradition, St. Ursula and 11,000 other virgins were put to death by the Huns near Cologne, Germany, and their martyrdom miraculously saved the city from conquest.

around Attila; it was they who attached the term *Scourge of God* to the Hunnic king, even though it was originally coined by St. Augustine for the Visigoth Alaric, who sacked Rome in A.D. 410. Once this transfer had taken place, however, it became the centerpiece of the Roman church's anti-Hunnic propaganda.

At some point in his career Attila himself must have found out that the Christians were calling him the Scourge of God, and apparently he never objected to it. The epithet probably appealed to his vanity, and he could also use it as a weapon to frighten the Christian world into submission.

The anti-Hunnic religious legends were consciously fabricated to spread the image of a cruel and destructive Attila. Yet not even they could always conceal the fact that behind this cruel bearing

103

French and Italian religious legends emphasize the victory, through divine intervention, of unarmed Christians over pagan warriors. In this painting, St. Geminianus (upper left) orders Attila and his Huns to halt their attack on the central Italian city of Modena. Allegedly, the city was spared when God rendered the Huns temporarily blind.

there was also a more noble, more courtly, and more humane Attila. This is evident, among others, from the Italian legend about a widow who was so despondent about her husband's death that she wished to commit suicide and take with her in death her 10 orphaned daughters. When Attila learned about this, he not only prevented this suicide but also presented the widow and her children with rich gifts. There is also the legend of the poet Marullus of Padua, who in his desire to flatter the conqueror, compared Attila to God. This sacrilege so enraged the king that he wanted to have the poet burned at the stake. In the end, however, Attila permitted Marullus to escape with his life.

While Christian-Roman religious legends are unabashedly anti-Hunnic, pagan-Germanic heroic epics painted two distinct and very contradictory portraits of Attila. South Germanic traditions describe him as a benevolent, friendly, and noble ruler, who at times was even too modest for his own good; Scandinavian or North Germanic traditions portray him as a shrewd, insidious, money-grubbing, and untrustworthy tyrant.

The first of these portraits is incorporated into such heroic epics as the 9th-century Song of Hildebrand, the 10th-century Walther's Song, and the 12th-century Song of the Nibelungs. Known as King Etzel, Attila is described in these Germanic epics as a peaceful, mostly inactive, and somewhat weak medieval king. He is also shown as a model husband and father, who is perhaps more under the thumb of his forceful queen than is good for him and his nation.

The best description of the Scandinavian-Germanic portrait of Attila, where he is known as Atil, is found in the 9th-century Song of Atil. Here, the king's environment is much more primitive than in the South Germanic epics; in the Atildichtung (Song of Attila), Attila is portrayed amid tribal circumstances, still ruled by a complex set of blood feuds.

Just as in the case of the propagandistic Christian legends, none of these German images reflects the true historical Attila. To a lesser degree, this

The Magyars, led by Árpád (mounted at right), followed in the footsteps of Attila and invaded Pannonia in the 9th century. The Magyars' claim of descent from the Huns became an integral part of Hungary's national legacy.

also holds true for the Hungarian historical traditions. In the Hungarian epics and chronicles, Attila's idealization is simply carried too far. In general, however, if one removes these elements of overidealization, the Hungarian image of Attila — that of a fierce equestrian warrior out to build an empire of continental proportions for his people — is probably closer to the truth than either the Western Christian, the German, or the Scandinavian image.

It is important to remember that conquest has traditionally been viewed as evil only by those who have fallen victim to it. Thus, while a conqueror was a hero in the eyes of his own people, he was always the embodiment of evil to those whom he conquered. And this applies just as much to such "civilized" conquerors as Alexander the Great, Julius Caesar, Charlemagne, or Napoleon as it does to such "barbarians" as Attila, Genghis Khan, Tamerlane, or Süleyman the Magnificent.

Attila's bad name in Western history, therefore, is due less to the merits of the case than to the fact that he lived in an age when the learned fathers of the Western church viewed all pagans on the borders of Christianity with suspicion. Attila's name and fame fell victim to the church's ideological struggle against paganism. The depth and extent of this negative Western image is best demonstrated by a survey commissioned a few years ago by *Time* magazine. A select group of professional historians — although few of them were experts in Hunnic history — was asked to list the 10 most hated personalities in history. Most of them included Attila, and many of them placed him close to the clear winner, Adolf Hitler.

But in the end, Attila the Hun was neither worse nor better than most of the great conquerors in world history. Like most of his fellow conquerors, he was obviously driven by a mission, and like all conquerors, he tried to achieve this largely through the use of arms. In the course of his conquests many innocent people died on both sides. But Attila has never been accused of killing for the sake of killing nor of having ever singled out a nation for extermination. As a matter of fact, his empire was a multinational and multireligious state, where one's origin made no difference in one's advancement; only one's capabilities mattered.

This is the reason that the ranks of his immediate advisers and military commanders included at least as many Germans, Sarmatians, Romans, and people of other nationalities as they did Huns. And this is also the reason that his former subject nations, among whom the various Germanic tribes were the most numerous, remember him rather fondly. To them, Attila was not a vicious barbarian but rather a great and gracious leader who lived a simple life, was fair and just to everyone, appreciated talent, and rewarded people on the basis of merit instead of birth. And to the Hungarians, of course, Attila represents much more than that. Although modern scholars reject a direct link between the Huns and the Hungarians, no one can eradicate from the collective Hungarian mind the belief in their Hunnic roots.

> *Good-bye my beloved country,*
> *Good-bye oh magnificent land,*
> *Region of the Tisza and*
> *the Maros rivers,*
> *Thou beloved homeland*
> *of my valiant people!*
> *I bequeath to thee my*
> *body and all my hopes,*
> *And I bequeath my soul*
> *to the gods in heaven,*
> *So that I may soar*
> *upon the firmament,*
> *And watch over you*
> *from the stars.*
> —GEZA GARDONYI,
> Attila's death song from the
> novel *The Invisible Man*

Further Reading

Gordon, C. D. *The Age of Attila: Fifth Century Byzantium and the Barbarians.* Ann Arbor: University of Michigan Press, 1960.

Grousset, René. *The Empire of the Steppes: A History of Central Asia.* New Brunswick, NJ: Rutgers University Press, 1970.

Jordanes. *The Gothic History of Jordanes.* Princeton: Princeton University Press, 1915.

Macartney, C. A. *The Medieval Hungarian Historians: A Critical and Analytical Guide.* Cambridge, England: The University Press, 1953.

Maenchen-Helfen, Otto J. *The World of the Huns: Studies in Their History and Culture.* Berkeley: University of California Press, 1973.

Seredy, Kate. *The White Stag.* New York: Viking, 1937.

Thompson, E. A. *A History of Attila and the Huns.* Oxford: Clarendon Press, 1948.

Wass, Albert, ed. *Selected Hungarian Legends.* Astor Park, FL: Danubian Press, 1971.

Wess, Roberts. *The Leadership Secrets of Attila the Hun.* New York: Warner Communications, 1987.

Wolfram, Herwig. *History of the Goths.* Berkeley: University of California Press, 1988.

Chronology

Index

Steven Béla Várdy is a professor of history at Duquesne University, adjunct professor of east European history at the University of Pittsburgh, former visiting scholar at the University of Budapest and at the Institute of History of the Hungarian Academy of Sciences, and the author or coauthor of more than a dozen books on Hungarian and east-central European history. His best-known works include *Modern Hungarian Historiography, Clio's Art in Hungary and Hungarian America,* and *The Austro-Hungarian Mind.* He is also the author of *The Hungarian Americans* in Chelsea House's THE PEOPLES OF NORTH AMERICA series.

Arthur M. Schlesinger, jr., taught history at Harvard for many years and is currently Albert Schweitzer Professor of the Humanities at City University of New York. He is the author of numerous highly praised works in American history and has twice been awarded the Pulitzer Prize. He served in the White House as special assistant to Presidents Kennedy and Johnson.
